Governing Illinois

Of the People,
by the People, and
for the People

N

Governing Illinois

Of the People, by the People, and for the People

Edited by
James M. Banovetz and Caroline A. Gherardini

Illinois Issues
Sangamon State University
Springfield, Illinois

This publication was made possible with support from the Illinois State Board of Education. Partial funding of printing costs was provided by First Chicago Corporation, IBM of Central Illinois, and Illinois Tool Works, Inc.

Appreciation is noted here for the ongoing commitment to this book by the *Illinois Issues* advisory board and especially the effort and time contributed by James M. Banovetz.

Printed in the United States of America on recycled paper.

Cover photo by: Bill Foreman, Silver Images Photography
Contributions of other photographs and artwork are listed alphabetically under "Illustration Credits," on pages 97 and 98.

Library of Congress Cataloging-in-Publication Data

Governing Illinois : Of the people, by the people, and for the people / edited by James M. Banovetz and Caroline A. Gherardini.
p. cm.
Includes bibliographical references and index.
Summary: Describes the system of state and local government in Illinois, emphasizing the functions and operation of the legislative, executive, and judicial branches.
ISBN 0-9620873-6-X
1. Illinois—Politics and government—Juvenile literature.
[1. Illinois—Politics and government.] I. Banovetz, James M.
II. Gherardini, Caroline A.
JK5716.G68 1991
320.4773—dc20

91-23544
CIP
AC

To order this book, write or call:
Illinois Issues
Sangamon State University
Springfield, Illinois 62794-9243
Telephone (217) 786-6084
FAX (217) 786-7257
Single copy, $10; 2-10 copies, $7.50 each; 11 or more copies, $6.50 each.

Foreword

This book about Illinois state and local government was designed and written for students in grades eight through twelve by some of Illinois' best school teachers. Its pages reflect the talents of these teachers supplemented by the expertise of the Illinois State Board of Education and *Illinois Issues*, the magazine of Illinois government and politics published cooperatively by Sangamon State University and the University of Illinois.

Illinois law has long required middle and high school students to demonstrate their knowledge of the Illinois Constitution and system of government. This book has been specifically prepared to help students learn about their Illinois government and politics.

James M. Banovetz and Caroline A. Gherardini, *editors*

Acknowledgments

For preliminary development:
Betsy A. Plank, member, *Illinois Issues* board
J. Michael Lennon, publisher, *Illinois Issues,* and executive director, Institute for Public Affairs, Sangamon State University
Dr. Sally Pancrazio, chair, Department of Educational Administration and Foundations, Illinois State University

For editorial planning and review:
Margaret Allan, Greenville Junior High School (Illinois Teacher of the Year, 1988-89)
William B. Branch, Evanston High School (Illinois Teacher of the Year, 1990-91)
Samuel K. Gove, professor and director emeritus, Institute of Government and Public Affairs, University of Illinois, and member, *Illinois Issues* board
Michael H. Hudson, vice president for public affairs, Illinois Tool Works, and chair, *Illinois Issues* board
Joan W. Levy, former president, Illinois Association of School Boards, and member, *Illinois Issues* board
David Parish, Beardstown High School
Ann Pictor, State Board of Education
Jack R. Van Der Slik, professor and director, Illinois Legislative Studies Center, Sangamon State University

For participating in field tests of the book:
Vincil Carter, Albany Park Multicultural Academy, Chicago
Patton Feichter, Maine Township High School, Park Ridge
William R. (Randy) Fritz, Williamsfield High School, Williamsfield
John Gustafson, Lincoln Middle School, Rockford
Phyllis Henry, Roberto Clemente High School, Chicago
John F. Huff, Greenville High School, Greenville
Dr. Mary Lee Lasher, Albany Park Multicultural Academy, Chicago
Milton Nelson, Maine Township High School, Park Ridge
Margaret Pierce, Steeleville High School, Steeleville
Dr. Philip Pogue, Greenville High School, Greenville
Colby Vargas, New Trier East High School, Winnetka
Barbara Young, Holy Cross School, Champaign

For special assistance to the editors:
C. Brooke Beal, assistant director, Solid Waste Agency of Northern Cook County
Kathleen A. Jaskowiak, assistant to the village administrator, Village of Bartlett
Frank C. Kopecky, professor of legal studies and acting director for the Center for Legal Studies, Sangamon State University
Dr. David W. Scott, State Board of Education

and from the staff at Illinois Issues, Sangamon State University:
H. W. Devlin, Mark A. Devore, Charlene Falco, Charlene Lambert, Thomas E. Morris, Beverley Scobell, F. Mark Siebert, and **Jennifer Smith;**

and from the staff at the Division of Public Administration, Northern Illinois University:
Bobbie Horsman and **June Kubasiak**

For authors, please see "Authors" on page 95.

For graphics, please see "Illustration Credits," on page 97.

Contents

SPEED
55
LIMIT
YOU'RE TRYING TO TELL ME SOMETHING, AREN'T YOU?
ENFORCEMENT
CONGRESS

CHAPTER 1

The Political Process: Parties, PACs, and Political Campaigns

By Patrick J. Burns

State Legislature Makes High School Diploma a Requirement for a Driver's License

State Legislature Ups Entrance Requirements for Admission to State Universities

City Council Sets 11:30 PM Curfew for All under 19

Local School Board Raises Graduation Requirements

Local School Board Cuts All Athletics for Next School Year

If these headlines were in your local paper, would you be interested? Other than the fact that all of these changes would affect students, what else do they have in common? All report actions taken by state or local governments.

Frequently, news stories tell us that American students know little about their government. Such reports are usually accompanied by a listing of a few questions that students were unable to answer, such as: What great historic event occurred in the early 1860s? Who was the sixteenth president? In some cases Illinois students are asked to name their state legislators or to identify the subject dealt with in Article I of the Constitution of the state of Illinois. The implication of these reports is that all educated individuals should be able to answer these questions. Right now, you may be thinking, "I'll bet a lot of adults can't answer these questions either," or, "Who cares what happened in the 1860s or who was the sixteenth president?" It is impossible to remember all of the information contained in history books or government documents. If the students had been asked where answers to the questions could be found, the results of such surveys might have been different and perhaps more meaningful.

Referring back to the headlines at the beginning of this chapter, answer these questions: What can I do if the state of Illinois decides to take away my driving privileges? What can I do if the school board decides to cut athletics for next year? If you don't know the answers, you are not in a position to stand up for your interests.

In a democracy such as ours, those who understand how the government works can make it work for them; those who do not understand how it works find that it often works against them. You have a choice of whether you are going to be one of the people who makes things happen or one of those to whom things happen. Those of you coming from families that understand how the system works can exercise power and influence your community to make changes. If you feel you are being treated unfairly, you or your family will bring pressure to bear on those in authority to get a problem corrected. On the other hand, those who do not understand how the system works believe that they have no power to change any situation. They may complain a lot but take no action and wind up adapting to a situation even though they are dissatisfied. Others may feel so alienated from the system that they resort to antisocial or even criminal behavior.

The State Journal-Register

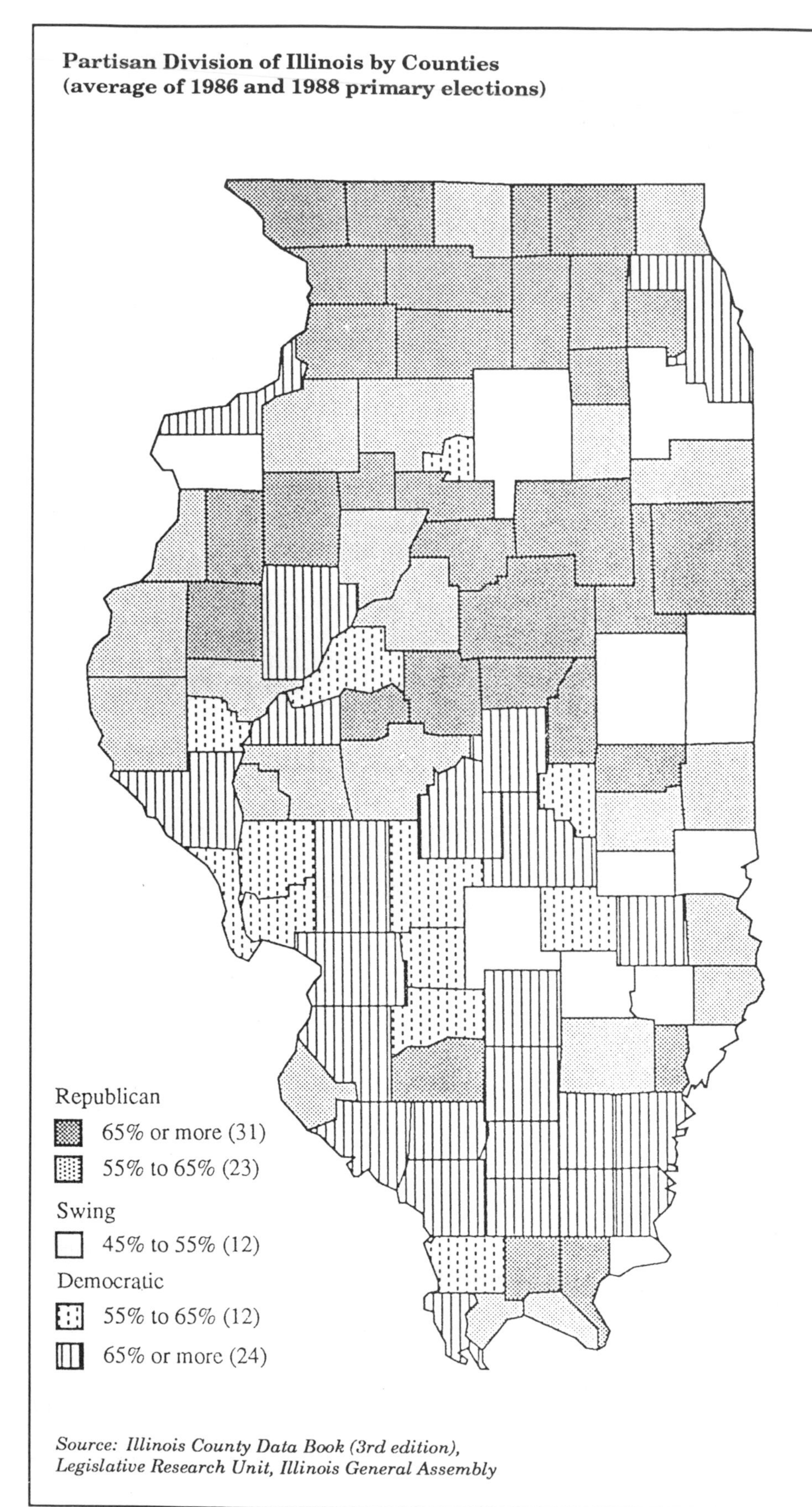

Power and Change

You may think that you have to be in a position of power before you can bring about changes. You may also feel that power is determined by money, skin color, or family background. While this view of power seems to have some truth, it is only partly true. If it were true today, blacks could not attend schools with whites; instead, they would sit in the back of the bus, they would not be served in "white" restaurants, and they would not hold political offices. All of these things were changed, not by those people in power at the time, but by people who learned how to make government work for them. The people in power changed afterwards because of new civil rights laws and court decisions. Of course, in a democracy, change may take a long time and lots of effort by people working together.

Take a look at the students in your school. Are there any girls wearing jeans? Do any of the boys have hair touching their collars? Are any of the boys wearing their shirttails outside their pants? Thirty years ago all of these were violations of the rules in most schools in Illinois, and students found to be in violation were subject to suspension. Are there any girls participating in interschool athletics? There weren't any thirty years ago. Have any of you attended a rock concert? Rock concerts were banned in many cities thirty years ago. Student activists of the sixties worked hard to get those changes made. Find out what rights you already have as a student because that is one of the first steps to understanding how government works.

Power and Politicians

Most of you are already aware of how state laws are written: Bills pass the legislature, are signed by the governor, and become law. Much more important to you, however, is understanding how to influence legislators and other government officials to pass or defeat bills.

To know how to pressure a legislator or other elected government official, consider what motivates them. Psychologists say that people want to be elected to a government office either because they enjoy feelings of power and prestige or because they enjoy helping others and wish to make the world a better place in which to live, or both.

Some of you may be thinking that an important reason was left out — money. While a desire for wealth may be a motivating factor for some people in public office, money is not a factor for most. Today, most people who have the ability to get elected to a government office can earn more money in other occupations. Some people who seek public office have already established successful careers. Many elected offices are part-time, especially for a city or a county or other local governments. Also note that many people seek elective positions which pay no salary at all. Members of your local school board are examples of people who, in most cases, receive no pay and usually serve from a sense of civic duty.

Politics is the art or science of influencing government; politics is also the art or science of winning election to a government office. Anyone holding an elected government position is also a politician. Some people enter politics and find that it is not at all what they expected. Perhaps they are uncomfortable using power, or they value their privacy more than the power and influence of the office. For whatever reason, these people do not continue in politics; however, for those who do enjoy politics and want to continue government service, their overriding goal becomes reelection. Special interest groups use the desire of politicians for reelection as a means of trying to get them to do what they want them to do while in office.

Political Parties

No understanding of the workings of Illinois government would be complete without a knowledge of partisan politics in Illinois. There are two major political parties in our state and nation — the Democrats and the Republicans. The National Democratic Party became very dominant during the 1930s by attracting blue-collar workers, minorities, poor voters, and intellectuals. The Democrats became closely allied with unions, and the union members voted for Democratic candidates. The Republican Party has tended more than the Democratic Party to be allied with industrial, commercial, and financial interests. The Republican Party traditionally contains many white-collar workers, professionals, business managers, middle-class citizens, retailers, and farmers, as well as the wealthy.

Regional and religious differences have been important in the political parties. Southern Illinois is more

The State Journal-Register / Sangamon Valley Collection, Lincoln Library

Faculty of Springfield Head Start Program, along with parents and their children, picket the Illinois Head Start and Day Care Association conference held in Springfield to show their dissatisfaction with the management of the local PACT (Parents and Children Together) program.

Democratic than northwestern Illinois for reasons that go back to the Civil War. For years, Catholics tended to be Democrats and Protestants to be Republicans. In the past few decades the parties have divided on social issues, and Republicans have gained among Catholics and white voters in southern Illinois.

Party politics in Illinois today is quite different from the old party politics of the 1930s and 1940s. Back then (before television), in Chicago and some other cities, the local precinct committeeman was the one to see for a job, food, clothing, or any of a wide variety of services that he would provide in exchange for your vote and the votes of your family in the next election. In rural areas, the same role was performed by the township supervisor. Today, the parties still sometimes use such officials as workers to get votes for their candidates, but, instead of such favors, they are more likely to use TV ads, computerized letters, and telephone calls to persuade voters to vote for a candidate.

Today, in Illinois, about one-fourth of its citizens and voters live in Chicago, which is in Cook County. Chicago votes Democratic, and the rest of Cook County, which has one-fifth of the Illinois population, splits half and half between Democrats and Republicans. Thus Cook County is dominated by Democrats. Another one-fifth of Illinoisans live in the affluent suburbs of the five collar counties around Cook — Du Page, Kane, Lake, McHenry, and Will — and vote mainly Republican. The

Bill Campbell

Dick Paulus

Dick Paulus

remaining third live throughout the rest of the state in the other ninety-six counties. While Cook County has been a Democratic stronghold, the collar counties have been just as strongly Republican. In a statewide election, such as for governor or one of Illinois' U.S. senators, these two groups tend to neutralize each other, and the winner is determined by the rest of the state.

Politics and Redistricting

Let's look at the rest of the state. First, remember that six counties around Chicago in northeastern Illinois have two-thirds of the state's people — and voters. The rest of the people in Illinois live in cities and towns and on farms spread from Rockford in the north to Cairo at the southern tip, from Quincy on the western border to Paris on the eastern border. Some areas are Democratic (like the Quad Cities and East St. Louis); others are Republican (like Peoria and Danville).

Now consider how members are elected to the Illinois General Assembly. The whole state is divided into fifty-nine Legislative Districts. The voters in each district elect a senator to the Illinois Senate. Each of the fifty-nine districts is further divided into two, creating 118 Representative Districts. Each of these elects one member to the Illinois House of Representatives. The boundaries for all these districts are redrawn every ten years after the U.S. Census is taken so each district is equal in population. The creation of those districts is not a simple mathematical division of the population. It is done in the General Assembly by the Democrats and Republicans who have all the voting records on computers. Democrats try to draw boundaries to increase the likelihood of electing Democratic senators and representatives, so their party will control the state legislature. Of course, the Republicans try to do the same.

Special Interest Groups

The senators and representatives elected to the General Assembly have loyalties to their parties and are accountable to the people in their districts. But there are also the special interest groups that cut across the entire state — and nation.

Who are these special interest groups? They are made up of ordinary people sharing a common interest; they are usually headed by people who understand government and how the political system works and how to make it work for them. For example, your teacher may be a member of a teachers' union: the Chicago Teachers Union or the Illinois Education Association/National Education Association (IEA/NEA) or the Illinois Federation of Teachers/American Federation of Teachers (IFT/AFT). These are special interest groups that work to influence politicians to support certain policies of interest to teachers, such as job security.

There are many special interest groups operating in Illinois, some more influential than others. Among them are those representing manufacturers, insurance companies, retail merchants, farmers, highway contractors, the medical professions, liquor distributors, realtors, and organizations representing most professional and labor groups, including the teachers' unions.

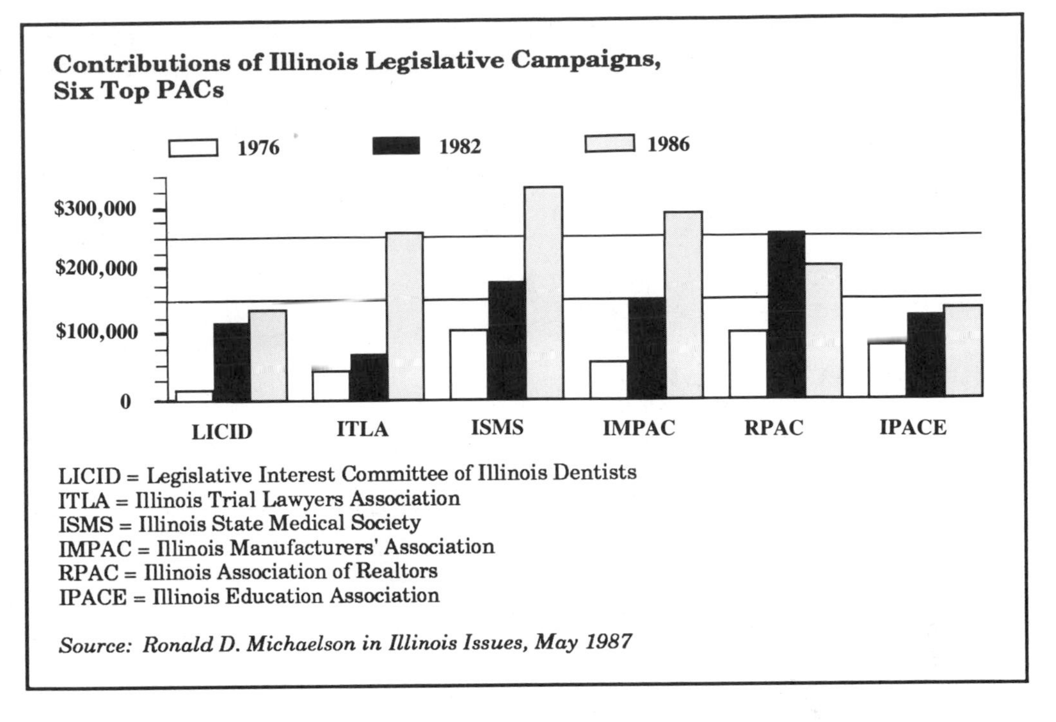

There are also interest groups representing African Americans, Hispanics, and other nationality groups.

In addition, there are powerful interest groups that are built around a single issue or a combination of issues that have little or nothing to do with a business or occupation. Examples of these groups and their issues are the National Rifle Association (NRA), the right of citizens to have guns; the American Civil Liberties Union (ACLU), protection or expansion of personal freedoms; the American Association of Retired Persons (AARP), economic benefits for retired workers; and the Angry Taxpayers Action Committee (ATAC), lower taxes.

Lobbyists and PACs

All of these special interest groups hire lobbyists, and many form political action committees called PACs. The job of lobbyists is to influence legislators to vote on bills in a manner favorable to their organization. Lobbyists provide a valuable service to legislators when they point out the advantages and disadvantages of various bills. They also help the legislator and other public officials by letting them know the desires of their constituents.

The PACs are the campaign funding arms of special interest groups. They use money and influence during election campaigns both to defeat candidates who vote or seem likely to vote against their interests and to help elect or reelect candidates who support their interests.

Many political scientists and political commentators are calling for laws which will prohibit or at least curtail the power of PACs. While PACs fit the concept of people working together to further their interests, unfortunately many Americans have no PAC to represent their interests. These same Americans are often less politically active. As a result, their interests tend to be given less consideration.

Students in Illinois colleges have a lobby group in Springfield, but students in schools do not. Without their own lobbyist or PAC, who then protects or expands rights for students in high schools, junior highs, and grade schools? Often, no one does. Sometimes, some of the special interest groups and their PACs may indirectly support positions favorable to students. For example, the ACLU has argued in court to protect or expand student rights.

Many of you may think getting a driver's license at age sixteen is the greatest event you can imagine. But at age eighteen you are granted a far greater power — the power to vote. Consider your future as a student in high school, college, or a business or trade school. Is

Bill Campbell

MOST OF IT REMAINS SUBMERGED – COMFORTABLE, SAFE AND OUT OF SIGHT.

Bill Foreman / Silver Images

Many a legislative deal has been cut "on the rail," the brass railing pictured here on the third floor of the Illinois Capitol. A crowd has gathered near the door to the House of Representatives at the top of the picture; directly below the photographer, the main door to the Senate is not visible. In the hectic final days of a legislative session, the rail is crowded with lobbyists hatching strategy, making final pitches to lawmakers, and talking politics.

there anything state government could do for you as a student? Public school students, represented by one giant organization, could become one of the largest special interest groups. Even if the students are not old enough to vote, with such a large number of students, modest dues would raise considerable money to hire a lobbyist and to fund a PAC. Such a lobby of even just Illinois eighth grade students might be in a position to influence such legislation as financial aid, minimum wage, and college entrance requirements.

Political Activity of Americans

Junior and senior high students are not the only group of people who have failed to form a special interest group to protect or advance their interests. Demographic surveys show that voting and political activism increase with age, income, and education. The least politically active are likely to be young, poor, and school dropouts.

Some Americans never even vote. They go through life without ever casting a ballot or even signing a petition or participating in a demonstration.

Some Americans vote regularly but take part in no other political activity such as contributing to a candidate's campaign or to a political party or even to a special interest group.

At the other end of the scale are political activists; they are deeply involved in political affairs on a regular basis. Most Americans, roughly forty-five percent, are not as consistent in their political activity: They may vote in some elections but not in others; occasionally they may be angry or upset enough to sign a petition, attend a board meeting, contact their legislator, participate in a rally, or contribute to a campaign or interest group.

It should come as no surprise that legislation enacted into law today tends to favor the politically active and their interests and causes because they have learned to make the system work for them.

Leaders or Representatives

Lobbyists who represent interest groups with powerful PACs have access to politicians and will be able to influence their votes and other political actions. Even so, such lobbyists cannot be sure of getting what they want. Often the interests of one group clash with the interests of others. How does a legislator decide which way to vote when interest groups are diametrically opposed on an issue? For example, an environmental interest group may want to ban throwaway bottles, but the bottling industry and retailers may oppose such a ban because it could cost them money.

After listening to the various views concerning proposed legislation, individual legislators must make a choice. They consider the views of their party and the people in their district. What do the voters want? On some issues, the legislator may have very strong convictions. If the legislator feels very strongly, he or she will lead the fight for the bill even though it is unpopular with powerful special interests or the legislator's party leaders or even constituents in the district. In this instance, the legislator is functioning as a leader, rather than as a representative. If legislators find themselves too often acting in opposition to positions taken by their party or interest groups that are powerful in their districts, they may find themselves in trouble at the next election.

Lobbyists know they will not win every legislator's vote; however, lobbyists cannot afford to lose too many votes or they may be out of a job. Lobbyists keep track of how legislators vote, and when reelection time comes, they have a list of "friends" and "enemies" ready for their PACs. All lobbyists and their organizations must register with the secretary of state.

The State Journal-Register / Sangamon Valley Collection, Lincoln Library

Several hundred people rallied on the east side of the Capitol in May 1989 to lobby legislators for increased education spending. Some signs pointed to Illinois' ranking of forty-fourth in per capita spending on education.

PACs and Campaigns

PACs flex their political muscle by giving campaign money to their legislator "friends." They also recommend that their members vote, and in some cases, perform campaign work for their "friends." Politicians who fail to support the position of the PAC will find that the campaign money and services will be withheld next time. Even worse, the money and services may be provided to their opponents.

It would be wrong to assume that PACs wait until the next election before they flex their political muscle. Just before important votes in the General Assembly, the PACs will have their members write letters and attend rallies in Springfield in favor of or opposed to legislation, depending on their position. Any group, not just PACs, can write letters and rally.

Personal letters, phone calls, and meetings have a major effect on politicians, whether they are state, local, or national. These methods added to rallies or demonstrations focus attention on an issue. Politicians in the General Assembly or on a city council, a county board, or a school board pay attention when citizens begin to show interest in an issue. An increase in political activity (letters, rallies, demonstrations) is a clue to the politician that continued and growing interest could mean citizens who did not vote in the last election will vote in the next. These additional voters could well change the outcome of the election.

Change in Political Parties

Political parties play a major role in state elections and in some local elections, but that role is not as important as it used to be. Traditional Republican voters increasingly view themselves as independents and do not vote a straight party ticket. Cook County Democrats are no longer united as they were under the late Chicago Mayor Richard J. Daley. Throughout the state the old Democratic coalition of blacks, ethnics, and union labor has split apart, too.

To some extent the Democrats are victims of their own success. They won collective bargaining, minimum wage, unemployment insurance, and workers' compensation. Also, workers in industry and the skilled trades now earn relatively high salaries; they live in nice homes, buy expensive cars, send their children to college, take expensive vacations, and, in general, do not think of themselves as blue-collar labor. With unemployment and wages less of a concern, their political interests turned to other issues such as crime, inflation, taxes, and abortion, on which the members of the coalition do not all agree.

While most political scientists applaud the demise of the party bosses and the "smoke-filled" rooms where a few people made major political decisions, the result has been a weakening of the two-party system and a separation of the average citizen from close involvement with a political party.

Bill Campbell

The State Journal-Register

Today the Democratic Party in downstate Illinois often finds itself at odds with Cook County Democrats on many issues, and the downstate Republicans do not always agree with the collar-county Republicans. In fact, on some issues downstate Democrat and Republican legislators vote together as a coalition in opposition to their northeastern Illinois counterparts.

While factions within each party may quarrel among themselves, they will usually work together to maintain control of the General Assembly. As a result, you may find a Democratic legislative leader from Cook County or a Republican leader from the collar counties providing financial help to a fellow party member from downstate who is involved in a close election. The favor may be repaid by delivering a crucial vote in the next legislative session in Springfield.

Ticket-Splitting

As the two parties weaken in the state and nation, not all voters claim to be either Democrats or Republicans. About forty percent today consider themselves independents. It used to be rare for voters to "split their tickets," that is, to vote, for example, for the Republican for governor and the Democrat for state senator on the same ballot. In 1964, only five percent split their vote between Democrats and Republicans. By 1978 forty percent split their vote.

It is this split-ticket voting that keeps one party from dominating. In 1991, Illinois Democrats held both U.S. Senate seats, a majority of Illinois' seats in the U.S. House of Representatives, and a majority in both chambers of the Illinois General Assembly. Yet, the Democrats do not control Illinois elections: The Republican presidential candidate nearly always wins the most votes in Illinois, and Republicans in the 1980s have usually held the offices of governor, lieutenant governor, and secretary of state — three of the six statewide executive offices.

It would be wrong to underestimate the influence of the political parties in a time of ticket-splitting. Most ticket-splitters still vote predominantly for one party and only cross over to vote for one or two people from the other party. Even independent voters are not completely independent: Most will lean toward one party or the other. Both political parties have PACs that raise a lot of money for campaigning, and they target it to win offices. They don't waste it on safe seats, where one party dominates a district. In general, Republican PACs ignore the city of Chicago races, and Democrat PACs ignore the races in the collar counties. What they don't ignore is an incumbent in trouble. Both parties conduct polls of voters and will jump in heavily if a poll shows that the incumbent is losing support.

Of course, other PACs are not completely partisan and will support candidates from either party, depending on who will vote their interests.

Campaigning for Reelection

Let's suppose a Democratic state senator with a strong pro-labor voting record is up for reelection in a district that could swing either Republican or Democrat. Both union- and business-oriented PACs will become involved in this race, as will the two political parties. This would be true even though incumbents are usually reelected. Incumbents have an edge because they are well-known in their districts. In addition, incumbents are likely to receive money from all of the PACs which were reasonably satisfied with their voting records.

The challenger, on the other hand, must develop name recognition among the voters. At the same time he or she must either convince voters who voted for the incumbent in the last election to switch their votes or persuade enough people who usually don't vote to go vote. In this example, Republicans and the business-oriented PACs will provide campaign money and services for the challenger. The first step in the challenger's campaign is to package and sell himself or herself to potential voters in much the same way as products are advertised. Television ads are key since they can reach most voters.

Frequently, a public relations firm will film the candidate and his or her family, trying to show that the candidate is interested in every voter in the district. If the district has a rural area, the candidate will be filmed wearing a seed company cap, leaning against some farm equipment, and talking to a group of farmers. If there are factories, the candidate will be filmed outside one wearing a jacket with a union logo. There will be other scenes: in front of an American flag, outside a church, on the street talking to members of the police force, or shooting baskets with a group of children. These scenes are put together, and a narrator's voice is recorded to add words to fit the idea of the pictures. The church and flag scenes will reflect "good old-fashioned" morals and patriotism; the farm and factory scenes reflect understanding of the needs of farmers and workers; the scene with the police officers suggests a commitment to law enforcement and public safety; the basketball scene contains a reference to the American competitive spirit. It doesn't matter that the candidate attends church only once or twice a year, has no farm background, knows little about law enforcement, has never held a union card, or has no athletic ability. The incumbent, of course, will be doing the same things.

If you're thinking that this is "dumb," that nobody would fall for this, remember commercials may seem "dumb" too, but they sell products. You know there is more to getting a date than the kind of shampoo you use or that eating a brand of cereal will not necessarily make you a champion. Nevertheless, this type of advertising sells products, and it sells candidates. Just as a wise consumer will not be unduly influenced by advertising, you, as a wise voter, should not be unduly influenced by campaign commercials.

Bill Campbell

SNAKE OIL

Illinois State Board of Education and Illinois State Board of Elections

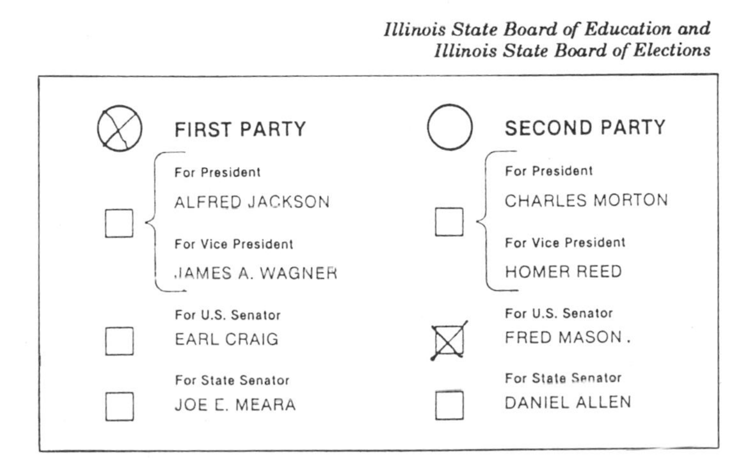

	FIRST PARTY		SECOND PARTY
☐	For President ALFRED JACKSON; For Vice President JAMES A. WAGNER	☐	For President CHARLES MORTON; For Vice President HOMER REED
☐	For U.S. Senator EARL CRAIG	☒	For U.S. Senator FRED MASON.
☐	For State Senator JOE E. MEARA	☐	For State Senator DANIEL ALLEN

This is a split ticket. Every candidate of the First Party except the candidate for U.S. senator is to receive one vote. Fred Mason, the candidate for U.S. senator under the Second Party, receives one vote. The vote in the square indicates the voter's specific intention to vote for Mason rather than Craig for U.S. senator.

The campaign staffs for both the incumbent and challenger will also send pamphlets and letters, writing separate ones to people with different interests such as farmers, workers, and business people. Selling their own candidate is not enough; they must also attack the opponent through negative campaigning. They will investigate the senator and his or her family for any evidence of wrongdoing. They will look at the candidate's voting record for inconsistencies and for votes on issues that could draw a special-interest PAC into campaigning against the senator. If found, the information is turned over to friendly reporters. For example, a vote for handgun registration could bring in the National Rifle Association. One relatively new technique is to find a particularly unfavorable photo of the incumbent and use it in contrast to the best possible photo or film clip of the challenger.

Everything described so far is legal and acceptable campaign practice, but some campaign managers resort to what are called "dirty tricks." If they find no evidence of wrongdoing, they manufacture some against the opponent. Campaign workers spread these derogatory rumors or charges about the opponent by word of mouth, claiming they come from an unnamed but very knowledgeable source.

Campaign Issues

You will note that nothing was said about the issues of labor and management in this imaginary campaign. Political campaigns do not often deal with in-depth discussions of the issues. The price of ads in the media

The State Journal-Register

The State Journal-Register

The State Journal-Register

makes it quite expensive for a candidate to cover any topic in detail. News reports in the media may be very brief, and candidates tend to make the same speeches, tailoring them for different audiences but providing no "news" to report in newspapers or on the radio or television.

Voters seem to prefer simple answers to complex problems and are confused or bored by long TV or radio discussions or news stories on issues. In addition, since every political decision that benefits one group of voters will be harmful to another, politicians prefer to remain vague about controversial issues. A tax cut is a popular position for candidates to take during a campaign; however, if voters find out that the cut is going to result in a major reduction in services, they may not want it. Think of your school. If a tax cut results in athletics being cut, those of you interested in athletics would be angry while others might not care. If the music program, the vocational program, or the college-prep program is cut, a different group of people would be angered in each instance. Politicians prefer to let the voters think the other person's program will be cut. Tax increases are rarely popular campaign positions unless voters feel they can count on them to pay for what they want.

Summary

You now have some idea about how the political system operates. As you read this book you will learn much more about government in Illinois. You will learn how government and politics work so you can make them work for you. It is your choice.

CHAPTER 2

The Powers and Duties of Government: How People Fit In

By Eleanor Meyer

Ban on Import of Assault Weapons Is Now Permanent

Asbestos Removal in Schools Almost Completed

Governor Signs Income Tax Legislation

Abortion Protesters Are Undeterred

Landfill Operator Fined for Violating EPA Standards

Power Company Rate Increase Approved by Illinois Power Commission

Citizens Comply with Restrictions on Water Use

Illinois Town To Test Flag-Burning Ruling

You may be surprised to discover how much of the news has to do with something that was done by the government. It might be something that was done by the government in your community — your local government. Or, it could be news of a decision that was made by the state government of Illinois. Much of the news deals with issues which are the business of the national or federal government. All Americans are subject to the rules established by these three levels of government, and all the governments are accountable to the citizens who vote. This book focuses chiefly on your state government and the many ways in which it affects your life.

Maybe you're thinking, "I don't read newspapers for news. I only read the sports section and the comics." Or you might be saying to yourself, "Who cares about the government? It's boring." Yet the government has influence in almost every aspect of your life. It is through the media—newspapers, television, radio, and magazines —that citizens can be informed about government activities.

If the government could control the media, we would only see and hear about the things the government wanted us to know. Freedom of the press, therefore, is one of our most cherished rights. Thomas Jefferson felt so strongly about this freedom of the press that he said, "... were it left to me to decide whether we should have a government without newspapers, or newspapers without government, I should not hesitate a moment to prefer the latter" (Letter to Col. Edward Carrington, January 16, 1787, *Bartlett's Familiar Quotations*).

This book was written with the hope that you will develop new attitudes about government. It is important for you to realize that government affects your life every day in every way. Once you understand the importance of government, you will see why democracy

The State Journal-Register

The aerial photograph shows the Springfield Capitol Complex surrounding the domed Capitol. Taken in the spring of 1989, the photograph is looking northwest and shows the Willard Ice Building, which houses the Department of Revenue, at the top and the Governor's Mansion in the lower right corner. The new State Library is to the right of the Capitol.

Dick Paulus

Dick Paulus

is only truly successful when all of its citizens are aware of the important part they must play in making that government work. If this book is truly successful, you will want to become involved and participate in the democratic process right away rather than at some vague time in the future.

Illinois State Government

The state government of Illinois. What do those words mean to you? Is the state government something that you know is real, but it seems far away? Is it a vague idea in your mind about a group of people who meet in Springfield and make decisions about things which you don't think you understand? Perhaps you think of government as a PLACE — a place where laws are made and taxes are collected and spent. Or do you think of state government as "those politicians" in Springfield who haggle and argue a lot and who don't seem to get anything done until the last days of June?

Kevin Jones / Senate Democratic Staff

Keeping in touch with constituents, Sen. James Rea of Christopher (Democrat, 59th District) talks with coal miners before they go to work at Zeigler Coal Company in West Frankfort.

If you have some of those ideas about your government, it means that you need to get a clearer picture of what government is all about. You need a way to make it seem less complicated. So let's begin with why we need government in the first place.

Why Do We Need Government?

Stop for a moment and think about what your classroom would be like if there were no rules about your attendance, your promptness, your participation, your conduct, or your supplies. What if there were no regulations to control the length of the class, the course requirements, the number of students in the room, or the professional training of your teacher? Pretty soon there would be chaos, right? If you belong to a ball team or a club at school, there are rules which govern your participation. Common sense tells us that without rules time is wasted, work is not done, goals are not attained, and confusion reigns.

Running the state is somewhat similar to running the classroom or the school. In a way, you and your classmates are a microcosm of the state. A microcosm is a little world that is typical of a larger world. The students in your class are a mixture of people of different sizes, shapes, and backgrounds. They have different cultural backgrounds and beliefs and different desires and attitudes. The same is true of the rest of the people in Illinois, and there are over eleven million of them. Just as your school would be a mess if there were no rules and regulations to guide people, the state would be very disorderly without some plan for managing it.

That is what state government does. It provides a

plan and a set of rules for everyone who lives in Illinois. Someone needs to set standards, for example, for such things as water treatment (to be sure that we have clean water to drink), sewage disposal (to be sure our sewage does not make people sick), and education (to see that education is available to every person of school age). It simply makes sense for the state government, which acts on behalf of all the people, to do those jobs. The state also establishes criminal codes as a means of regulating individual behavior.

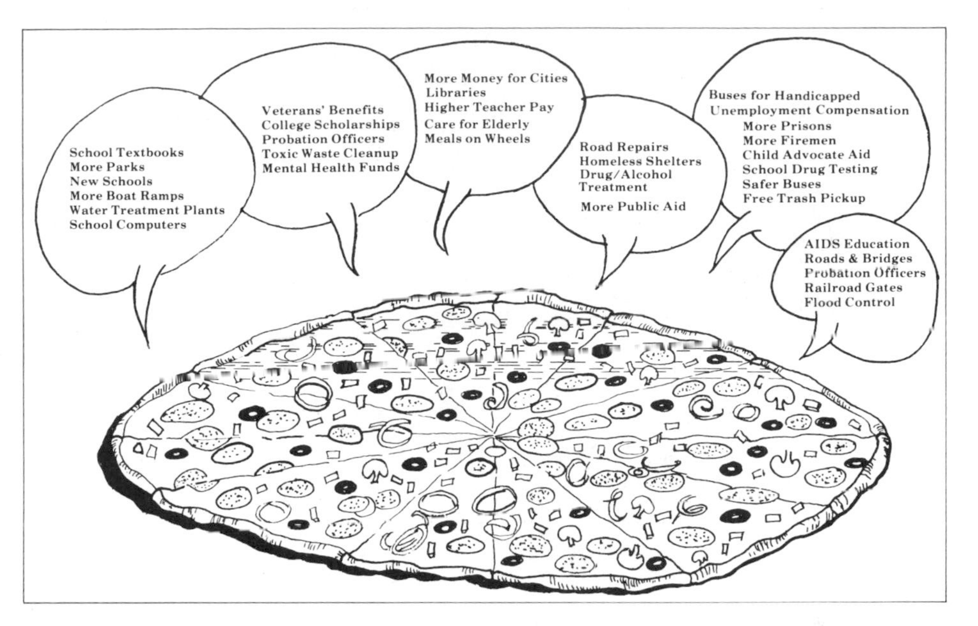

The government, in turn, must also operate under a set of rules to make sure it does what the people want. Maybe the Illinois State Constitution will seem less complicated to you if you think of it as the set of rules under which the government operates. That Constitution was written by people elected as delegates from across the state, and the Illinois Constitution was ratified or approved by its citizens in a statewide election.

How Are Decisions Made?

The rules in the Illinois Constitution provide us with a framework for running our representative government in Illinois. There are powers and duties assigned to the executive, legislative, and judicial branches, just as there are in the U.S. Constitution for the federal government. The voters in your district elect a representative and a senator to go to Springfield to work for your interests just as they elect someone to go to Washington, D.C., to work for the interests of Illinois in the U.S. Congress.

But don't forget, when the Illinois General Assembly makes decisions, it makes them for all the people in all the districts, and the state representatives and state senators often have tough choices to make. Maybe your student council has been in a similar situation. They had successful fundraisers, and then they had to decide how to use the money. Some members may have wanted to buy computer equipment, others may have wanted lab equipment, and perhaps some thought they deserved to spend some of the money on themselves. Any representative group will spend time debating, arguing, soul-searching, and finally compromising before the final vote is taken.

Think how much more complicated a state legislator's job must be, especially in a state as diverse as Illinois. Illinois is both agricultural and industrial; it is urban and rural; it is cosmopolitan and provincial. It has great wealth as well as areas of great poverty. Each district in the state has special needs for which it wants state help. Your home district might need money for new roads while another might want a prison built so that new jobs will be created. Some areas of the state desperately need more money to keep their schools going. The list of demands is long. Yet the state cannot spend money it does not have.

What if everyone in your family had the same birthday? What would be the chance of your getting the presents you wanted? In a way, that's the way people are about their government. They expect the government to give them what they want, and they expect their representatives to find a way to get it.

Deciding Where the Money Goes

There's more to it. In addition to trying to meet the needs of all regions of the state, the General Assembly must make its decisions with a budget in mind. There is just so much money to spend but many, many ways to spend it. You've seen those pie graphs that show how much money is available and where it goes.

You might appreciate how tough it is to decide how to allocate all that money if you would use your imagination and turn that budget into a pizza. Put yourself in the impossible situation of having to feed twenty-five people with a pizza that is large enough for just twelve servings. How do you decide who gets a slice? Do you give the most to those who are pushiest? Do you deny it to those who got there late? Do you cut it up in very small pieces so that everyone gets some but no one really satisfies his or her appetite?

The state budget is like that pizza. Just as there is only so much pizza to be divided, so too is there only so much money to be divided by the government. While the

Terry Farmer / Showcase Photography

Rock Island's Alleman High School met Springfield's Griffin High School (now Sacred Heart-Griffin) in a game in 1987. As with public schools, private schools like Griffin and Sacred Heart are often forced by increasing costs and decreasing enrollments to consolidate.

national government can — and does — operate with a deficit, that is, it spends more money than it takes in during a year, the state cannot do that. Article VIII of the Illinois Constitution requires that state government's spending plan for one year cannot exceed state government's estimate of the money it will get in that year. Citizens must realize that the state government cannot solve all problems by spending more money — it can only spend the money it receives in a year, mainly from taxes paid by citizens. If government spends more, it must tax more.

Determining how to divide the money in the state budget is something like the problems with the pizza. There is just so much money to spend. There are hundreds of ways to divide it. There are lobbyists who try to persuade legislators to spend it for their special interest group. Those groups might include farmers, lawyers, doctors, insurance companies, health agencies, welfare recipients, teachers.

There are 118 state representatives and fifty-nine senators who are responsible for making the budget decisions. They should keep in mind what the Preamble to the Illinois Constitution says about providing "... for the health, safety and welfare of the people ..." and about eliminating "... poverty and inequality ..." and about assuring "... legal, social, and economic justice ...." If you were a legislator, how would you decide to vote if you had to choose between providing aid to the ever-growing numbers of elderly citizens who need long-term care and the growing demand for government-funded day care for children of working mothers? Now, how do you vote? Which group will support you in the next election because of the way you voted?

Government of the People, by the People, and for the People

Do you still think government is boring? Are you at least beginning to see that it is not some vague "thing." It is people, and they are very real and very active. Every bill that is read in the General Assembly begins with these words: "Be it enacted by the people of Illinois represented in the General Assembly ...." This reminds us that the legislature is doing its business with the consent of the governed, that is, the citizens of Illinois. It reminds us, as Abraham Lincoln did over 100 years ago in his Gettysburg Address, that this truly is a government "of the people, by the people, and for the people." Those words are meaningless if the people — you — do not think it is important to understand how the system works. It was Aristotle who said: "If liberty and equality ... are chiefly to be found in democracy, they will best be attained when all persons alike share in the government to the utmost" (Politics III, *Bartlett's Familiar Quotations*).

Government Enters Your Life

Let's look at some of the ways in which government directly affects your life. You started school at the age that is set by the state. If you attended preschool or nursery school, the state had rules about how that school was run. People who run such schools have to be licensed by the state. To attend school, you had to be inoculated against certain contagious diseases. This protects not only you; it protects the rest of society as well because you will not be a carrier of those diseases. If you participate in any school athletic programs, you

Thomas Roth / Illinois State Police

Illinois State Police Trooper Bill Emery makes many visits to Illinois classrooms to tell young people about the D.A.R.E. (Drug Abuse Resistance Education) program. In 1990, officers taught the D.A.R.E. program in almost 1,200 public and private elementary schools in Illinois and expanded the program to senior high schools. The officers estimate their message reaches over 250,000 children each year.

know that you had to have a physical exam before you could play. It's the law.

You may question the state's right to interfere in your personal life, but remember, the Preamble to the Illinois Constitution says that we are committed to "provide for the health, safety and welfare of the people." Since the law requires you to attend school, the state has an ideal place in which to reach all of the children and to take steps to protect their health.

The government also has some control over what you should be taught in school. Just as this class is designed to educate you to understand and appreciate your system of government, the school must offer health classes which point out the risks involved in experimenting with drugs and using tobacco and alcoholic beverages. Addiction to drugs not only affects health; it also leads to crime and the breakdown of families. All of society suffers when its families and especially its children are in trouble. Many teenagers, as you know, are becoming parents too soon. By providing information to students at an early age, the state hopes to help young people to make wise choices even though they live in a world in which drinking, smoking, taking drugs, and engaging in sex are made pretty appealing sometimes on TV and in movies and magazines.

While each individual has wide freedom to choose the lifestyle he or she wants, society can provide the means for helping the individual make an educated choice. In a democratic society, where the powers of its government are derived from its citizens, it is important for the citizens to be literate and able to support themselves and their children.

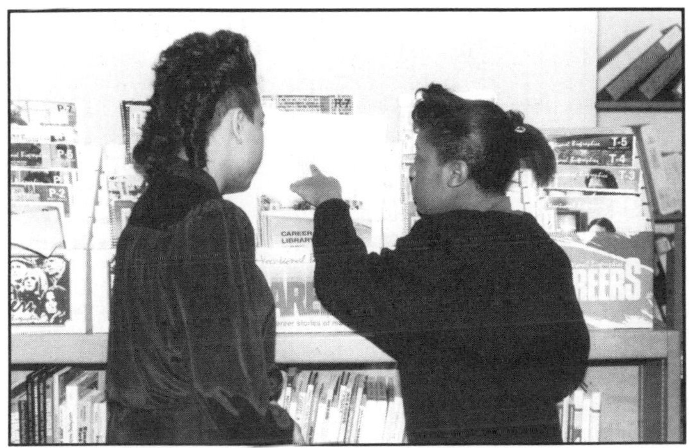

Illinois Department of Public Aid

Project Pride, a pilot program of the Illinois Department of Public Aid, offers young women in Joliet West High School an opportunity to enter the job market while completing high school. Participants receive help with their courses so they can graduate, and they experience the "real world" problems, responsibilities, and feelings of satisfaction that go with having a paying job.

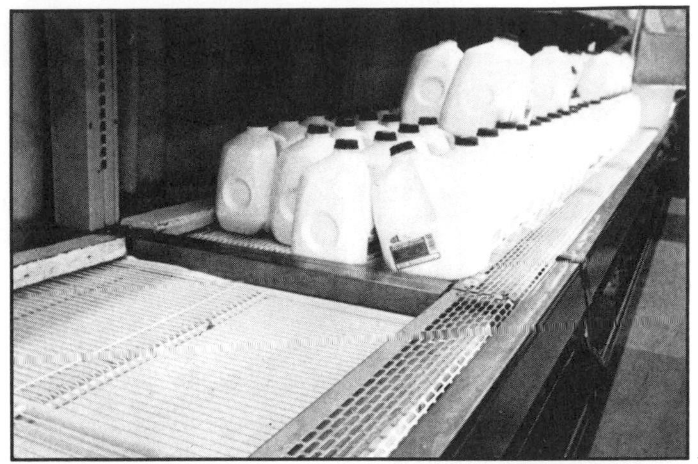

Jan Abbott / Herald and Review

In April 1985 milk from certain dairies in Illinois was removed from store shelves as a precautionary measure to protect the public from salmonella poisoning. Although milk is rarely a source for salmonella bacteria, the 1985 outbreak in Illinois is the largest ever recorded in U.S. history. According to the Department of Public Health, salmonella bacteria are most often found in eggs and poultry.

Government and Your Health

Here is another example of the way government looks after the health of its citizens. In 1985, 17,000 Illinois residents were sickened by drinking milk that contained a bacteria known as salmonella. Six people died. Imagine the detective work it took to trace the brand of milk to a particular dairy. The state's Department of Public Health is equipped to handle such emergencies. This agency also had the authority to shut down that dairy until the owners complied with sanitation guidelines for producing milk that was safe to drink. The state provided instructions for the victims so that they could take the necessary steps to keep the disease from spreading. The crisis would have continued to spread if there had not been a government department that was trained and prepared to cope with the situation. You and your family were protected by government action.

Don't Take My Driver's License!

If you still cannot see that government influences your life every day, it might help to think about one of your cherished possessions — your driver's license. Even if you are not yet old enough to drive, you probably have daydreamed about getting behind the wheel and taking off — legally. Since driving is a serious responsibility, the government has determined you must be sixteen years of age before you take the tests that allow you the privilege of a driver's license. Of course, there are rules to be followed so that the roads and highways are safe for all citizens. There are state, county, and local police to enforce these rules. All of this comes under the responsibility of government.

Photos by Terry Farmer / Showcase Photography

Driver's license facilities, like the one near the Capitol in Springfield at 316 North Klein (top), are located in cities throughout the state. Motorcyclists (center) must pass a "road test" just as automobile drivers do, and everyone must pass a vision test (bottom) in addition to a written test on the *Rules of the Road*. Driver's licenses are renewed every four years, and all drivers must pass the vision test before being issued a new license. Drivers also have to take the written test if they have had a moving violation—speeding ticket, accident, etc.—since their last renewal. Drivers are also chosen at random to take the written exam.

When some of these rules are violated too often, the state government, which issues driver's licenses, has the authority to tighten up on the regulations. For instance, the legal drinking age in Illinois used to be nineteen. When statistics showed that an overwhelming number of auto accidents were the result of teenage drinking and driving, the state, acting in the interest of the safety of all its citizens, changed the drinking age to twenty-one.

Illinois State Police

An Illinois State Police officer radios in to the Command Center from the shoulder of the road. In 1990, state troopers assisted almost 120,000 motorists on Illinois highways and investigated 56,500 accidents. Nine percent of the 1,900 uniformed officers and special agents in the Illinois State Police force are women.

Your license is not handed to you just because you passed Driver's Training. You must pay a fee for it, just as you had to pay for the permit which allowed you to take the instructions. The money that you pay when you get a license is one of the legitimate ways in which the government is able to raise money to do some of the things that it is expected to do.

The money from these fees is spent in many ways: It helps pay for the cost of testing applicants for driver's licenses, but some of the money is also used to help pay for such government services as the construction and repair of roads, driver education programs, and bicycle safety training programs. None of the money goes directly to the persons who conduct the driver's license tests or who issue your license to you. The money goes to the state treasury, and the salaries of these state workers, like all state employees, are set by laws and rules.

The state Constitution gives the Illinois General Assembly the power to raise money in various ways. Licensing fees, fines, user fees, and proceeds from the sale of state resources and bonds are all sources of funds, but taxes on what you buy (sales taxes) and on what you earn on a job (income taxes) are the major sources of money for state government. Local governments have the power to tax property. You will learn more about taxes in Chapter 8. There is an old saying that we can be certain of only two things in life — death and taxes. Nobody likes to pay taxes, but most citizens realize that we have to pay for all the services that we expect from our governments. Remember that pizza?

How Tax Dollars Reach Your Community

What are some of these services that people want and how do they reach from Springfield to your hometown? Before we answer that, it might help to think about the many categories of people in any community. There are children and adults. There are students, workers, and retired people (who may also be students). There are business people, farmers, veterans, Medicaid recipients, alcoholics, drug abusers, child abusers, other lawbreakers, and on and on. While every community may have its schools, restaurants, nursing homes, and stores, it may also have specialized services. Some have big shopping centers; others have large industries; some are farming communities, while others are centers for banking and professional services; still others have universities, hospitals, tourist attractions, or prisons. You get the idea — there is a great deal of variety and activity in every corner of Illinois.

What you may not realize, though, is that for all of those groups we just listed, some government agency or department is responsible for regulating, counseling, inspecting, or providing some type of service. Each of these agencies has offices and staffs. They print brochures and other materials to let the public know what is available through their offices. They might sound familiar when we tell you that these departments have names like Department of Agriculture, Department on Aging, Department of Children and Family Services, Department of Corrections. This is just a sample. Your teacher probably has a copy of the *Handbook of Illinois Government,* which tells more about them. (It is published by the Illinois Secretary of State.) You can also read more about them in Chapter 5 on the executive branch.

Terry Farmer / Showcase Photography

Farms such as this one in northern Illinois are served by programs administered by the Department of Agriculture. In 1989, Illinois had 86,000 farms on 28.5 million acres, which is eighty percent of its total area.

Photos by Terry Farmer / Showcase Photography

Employees in areas as diverse as industrial centers such as Peoria (above) and business centers such as Michigan Avenue in Chicago (below) are served by the Department of Labor, which makes sure Illinois' workers have a safe, healthy place to work and are paid wages in compliance with the state's minimum wage, overtime, one-day-rest-in-seven, Child Labor, and Industrial Homework laws. Between 1987 and 1990, the Department of Labor helped more than 100,000 workers collect payment of $80.3 million in unpaid and back wages.

The point is, these departments may have offshoots in your town or city, but you may not recognize them as part of the government. If your community offers programs on alcohol and drug abuse, if it provides homes for foster children, or if it gives assistance in the form of nursing care and meals for the elderly, then it is making use of state funds to provide for the "health, safety and welfare of the people."

Illinois Department of Conservation

Campers pay a fee to spend the night in Illinois state parks. This family is enjoying a Rent-a-Camp site maintained by the Department of Conservation. Most of Illinois' sixty-six state parks have camping facilities.

Illinois Department of Transportation

Maintaining the state's $60 billion highway network is the responsibility of the Illinois Department of Transportation. The state system of roads accounts for only twelve percent of the 137,516 miles of public roads in Illinois but carries approximately sixty-six percent of all traffic. Here workers are building a new portion of Route 99 near Mount Sterling.

Sometimes the state provides these services directly. For example, the state has hospitals which care for the mentally ill. Other times the state provides these services through a local government. Your county, for example, has a department of public aid to help the poor, and it is likely a not-for-profit agency such as a senior citizens center that provides programs to help elderly citizens. The idea is to make government services more readily available across the state.

The Three Main Levels of Government

There are many governments and government offices in Illinois, but they all fall into the three main levels — national, state, and local. It might help you to think about them as if they were the floors of a three-story building. The ground floor represents your local government. In a municipality, this might be a mayor and a city council or a village board of trustees. For your county it will be a county board that meets in the county seat. There are lots of other local governments on that ground floor in Illinois: townships, school districts, library districts, and airport authorities, for example. All are governments located in the community and run by local citizens.

The second floor of the building represents the state government. The state government offers some services directly. For example, it builds state highways and operates the prison system. State government also coordinates the efforts of local governments to be sure that other services such as public education are made available to every person in the state. The state government is the link between the bottom floor and the third or top floor, which is the national or federal government.

The federal government on the top floor also has certain powers and responsibilities. For example, it provides military protection, maintains our relationships with other nations, and helps state and local

Terry Farmer / Showcase Photography

Brenda Edgar holds the Grand Champion rabbit bought by the Edgars at the 1989 Illinois State Fair. The Department of Agriculture administers the State Fair at Springfield and the DuQuoin State Fair in southern Illinois.

Illinois Department of Corrections

A view of Stateville Correctional Center inside the wall. Stateville is a maximum security prison in Joliet. By mid-1992, the number of adult inmates in Illinois prisons is expected to exceed 32,300.

governments finance and provide housing, health, welfare, education, and many other programs for people.

The three floors are connected with stairs or elevators just as the three levels of government are linked through many of the agencies and departments that we have been talking about. Each floor supports the other, and the top floor would collapse without the support of the other two floors, just as the federal system would collapse without the support and participation of the people throughout the nation.

While it would still be possible for a single national government to run this country, it would be far less desirable than our federal system which leaves certain matters in the hands of citizens in the states and communities. If only a centralized national government existed, you would have to picture a huge building with no floors between the roof and the ground floor. There would be a vast space between bottom and top, just as there would be a great distance between local communities and their national government. Other nations don't have state governments. All powers reside in the central, national government, as in England.

These three levels of government sometimes affect your life in unlikely ways, and we are trying to convince you that you should care about that. Let's go back to one of the headlines at the beginning of this chapter, the one about the landfill operator who was fined for failing to follow some of the regulations set up by the Environmental Protection Agency. The headline is real and the topic is serious, so before you decide that it's time for you to "tune out," let's take a look at the part you play in this landfill problem — and you do play a part. We all do.

You, Your Trash, and the Government

Stop and think for a moment about the amount of trash and garbage you disposed of in the last twenty-four hours. Seriously, make a quick list. Chances are you pitched such things as gum and candy wrappers, styrofoam hamburger containers, cartons from your french fries, napkins, straws, and plastic cups. Have you ever thought about the mountains of cups that are thrown away every day in your town or city? In your state? In the entire country? And we are just talking about the cups! What about the disposable diapers, chicken bones, paper, bottles, and cans that we all toss in the trash? Some estimates say that sixty percent of what people carry home from the grocery store is packaging that is thrown away.

Illinois Department on Aging

At an information booth in the State of Illinois Center in Chicago a representative of the Illinois Department on Aging answers questions about services that allow the state's senior population to continue living independent lives.

Terry Farmer/Showcase Photography

The Assembly Hall at the University of Illinois serves many purposes, including athletic stadium and concert hall, that benefit the public as well as the university community. Illinois' public universities enroll nearly 194,000 students.

The State Journal-Register

Springfield Lake Area Disposal trucks empty lawn waste bags onto an open field just off Route 29. The field is used for composting the lawn wastes, which can no longer be dumped into landfills. A number of landfills have reported that they will have to close due to their inability to meet new regulations adopted by the Illinois Pollution Control Board in 1990. Of 117 commercial landfills listed in a 1990 Illinois Environmental Protection Agency report, twenty-nine will close earlier than previously reported, nine will close by 1997, and twenty will close in 1992.

Illinois Environmental Protection Agency

Household hazardous waste is a growing environmental concern. Some of the chemicals, paints, and sprays stored in our homes are hazardous but cannot be easily disposed of safely.

Everything you throw out must be dumped someplace. Today we call those dumps "landfills." As more people throw out more trash, the amount of space required to dump the trash also increases. Illinois is running out of landfill space, and that is a problem that affects every single one of us. It is an example of the kind of problem that we tend to expect our government to take care of.

It makes us a little bit uncomfortable to think about the part we play in contributing to the problem of trash. Yet there is no ducking it — it is everybody's problem. It isn't going to go away; it is only going to get bigger. So let's take a closer look at the situation.

In many communities citizens must separate glass and paper products from their other household wastes. That's an example of a law made by local governments (usually called an ordinance). Illinois has a new state law (called a statute) that says citizens must separate landscape waste (leaves, grass clippings and tree limbs) from regular garbage. That's an example of the state law enforced through the Illinois Environmental Protection Agency. It has many other laws that follow standards set by the federal government through the U.S. Environmental Protection Agency. And that takes us back to the headline about the landfill operator.

When the landfill operator violated federal regulations for not handling refuse in a safe and proper way, he was fined. It was a state inspector who reported him. That's two of those levels of government exercising their powers in an area that affects all of us every day. Where does the third level, the local government, come into this? In order to show you that, we have to sidetrack briefly.

Americans are often described as a "throwaway society." We like things to be packaged for our convenience from our hamburgers to our records and tapes. We like things to be disposable from baby diapers to plastic bottles. At the same time, we want a clean, healthy environment. Some of us pressure our lawmakers until they do something about the terrible mess we are making of our environment. Facts and information are presented by experts and advocates for protecting the environment. Our lawmakers responded and today we have federal and state laws and agencies — the U.S. Environmental Protection Agency and the Illinois Environmental Protection Agency — whose job is to make and enforce rules according to the laws passed by our elected representatives to protect the environment. Good. We asked for it.

Trash—a Growing Problem

Back to the landfill operator. It used to be easier to run a landfill. New rules make it more complicated and more costly. Paying fines is not profitable, so many

The State Journal-Register

private landfill operators are getting out of the business. In 1980 there were 800 private landfills in Illinois; in 1990 there were fewer than 200. Here's where your local government steps in. Even though there are fewer landfills, your local government must still get rid of the trash you throw out.

In some communities the local government takes responsibility for picking up trash, and the citizens pay for this service through taxes. In others, private companies collect the trash for fees. No matter how it is handled, there are state and federal guidelines for waste disposal which must be followed. And the citizens, all of us, must expect to pay for this service which we all need and often take for granted.

This discussion of the problems of waste disposal is just one example of ways in which those levels of government affect all of us, every day, in a very basic way.

We used the example of trash disposal to explain the three levels of government because it is a problem that will still be around when you are old enough to vote. It is a national problem. Believe it or not, the state of New Jersey has a museum devoted to trash! The museum has displays that show how those plastic forks and soda bottles refuse to disappear after 100 years. There is even a magazine called *Garbage: The Practical Journal for the Environment.*

Problems Lead to Solutions

People are working on solutions to the problem, though, and government can help by providing money for research. Recycling centers are part of the solution. In Illinois, corn-based degradable plastic bags for solid waste disposal are being used in some cities. This solution has the added benefit of providing a new market for Illinois farmers.

Sometimes problems cause us to find solutions that bring extra benefits, such as the new market for corn for making the disposable bags. But all too often, solutions to problems are complicated by the attitudes of those who have created the problem in the first place. Existing landfills are filling up, and environmental regulations make it increasingly difficult to find new sites for landfills. As local governments struggle to find suitable locations for landfills, they run into the "NIMBY" problem. NIMBY stands for "Not In My Back Yard," and that is the position that is usually taken by property owners and neighboring communities when they hear that the government might establish a trash dump in their area.

Government Regulations Are Everywhere

Your garbage disposal system is only one example of a local government service that is affected by state and federal regulations. Government sets standards for water treatment plants, sanitary districts, pesticide use, utility rates, and building and highway construction, to name a few. Even cemeteries are governed by certain burial procedures! Actually, about seventy-five percent of the activities of your local government must comply with state and federal regulations.

Do You Want Progress or Not?

Just as it is easy to take our garbage collection for granted, it is easy to expect our roads and highways to be built and maintained for our convenience. Our nation is automobile-dependent. Look at the state highway map and see the countless number of roads that criss-cross Illinois. Billions of dollars are spent to build and maintain this system. All of the funding comes from

Terry Farmer / Showcase Photography

The corn harvested by this farmer near Petersburg could be processed into ethanol, a fuel that is not only cleaner to burn than petroleum products but also has the potential to produce jobs for Illinois agriculture and agriculture-based industries.

government — local, state, and federal.

Although the Tenth Amendment to the U.S. Constitution clearly gives states the right to make laws affecting their people, there are times when the federal government can use its muscle to influence state legislation. For example, if state laws do not comply with the federal government's laws on maximum speed limits or minimum drinking ages, the federal government can withhold funds for highway construction. The state could set a higher speed limit or lower its drinking age, but it will have to build all of its roads with its own money. No state can afford to lose this help. That is another example of state and federal powers.

The need for more highways creates some problems which are similar to the problems that accompany the need for more landfill sites. Many areas of this country are developing rapidly, and state and county officials try to ease the increasing traffic volume by working to enlarge two-lane roads to four-lane roads. That sounds reasonable enough, right? Yet the NIMBY attitude pops up again because many citizens don't want increased growth in their communities and neighborhoods.

There is continuing conflict between those who see growth and development as a positive force called progress and those who don't want growth and development because of problems they may cause. The debate may focus on new construction and jobs versus loss of open space and increased traffic congestion. Many people do not want to live on a four-lane road and will fight any attempt to make their street wider. Are you beginning to understand how difficult it can be for legislators to make decisions that satisfy people and at the same time protect the rights and meet the needs of people?

You Are Part of Government

By now, you should have a clearer idea of the ways in which government influences your life — every day. The chapters that follow will help you to understand more about how the government actually works. At this point, you should at least be able to recognize how much of the news and newspaper headlines have to do with government — local, state, and federal. When you are old enough to vote, age eighteen, you will have a power granted to you by the Twenty-Sixth Amendment to the U.S. Constitution. By the time you finish this book, you should realize that your own involvement is the key to better government.

CHAPTER 3

Constitutionalism: A Contract with the People

By Denny L. Schillings

Illinois state government and our national government have many things in common. Their constitutions are similar insofar as they establish a system of government, affirm citizen rights, and impose limitations on government. Both governments are republican in form because their decisions are made by officials elected by their citizens. They are also democratic governments because there are regular elections with decisions determined by majority vote, and the powers of the governments are vested in the people.

We are a nation of fifty state governments operating simultaneously with the national government in Washington, D.C. The only way it can work successfully is through cooperation. The document that establishes that cooperation is the U.S. Constitution.

When delegates from each state met in Philadelphia in the summer of 1787 to write a constitution for the nation, they faced a monumental problem: how to balance powers of individual states and powers of a central government serving the entire nation. Each of the states was worried about the loss of power to a centralized government with too much authority. The first attempt at a national government under the Articles of Confederation did not work very well for the United States of America. Our young nation lacked a strong central government, and the individual states were not cooperating with one another. The delegates in Philadelphia agreed that they had to craft a constitution to insure cooperation of states as a nation and at the same time protect the interests of the individual states.

Herald and Review

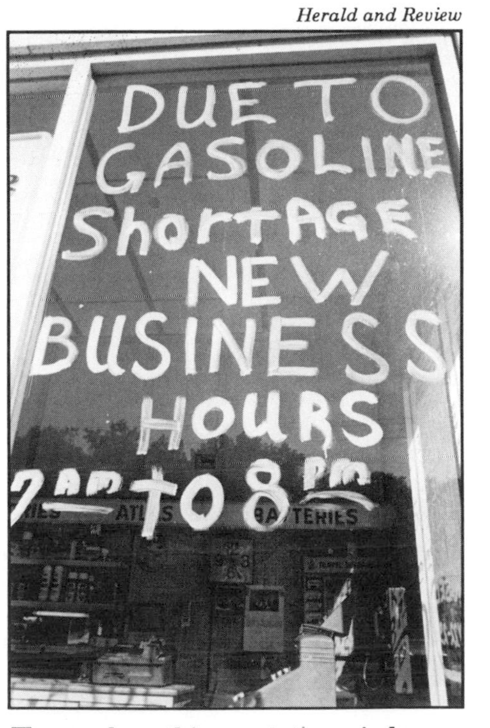

The words on this gas station window told a familiar story of gasoline shortages in 1973 in the United States. Arabian oil countries wanted higher prices, so they cut production. That resulted in too little supply to meet America's demand for oil.

Herald and Review

The 1973 oil shortages resulted in gasless gas stations like this one. When a gas station opened up, cars would line up for blocks. Gasoline prices went up, and people had to carefully plan how far they could drive their cars, so they wouldn't run out of gas.

The Concept of Federalism

Like most decisions made by the delegates, the problem of states' rights was dealt with through a series of compromises. The Constitution divides authority, giving the national government certain specific powers, reserving to the states other powers, and establishing that some authority is shared between the state and national governments. This system of government is called federalism.

While federalism explains the relationship of the states to the national government, it is a concept that can help in understanding the relationship between a state government and all its local governments. The Illinois Constitution establishes the central state government and the framework for local governments throughout the state. Basic local governments in Illinois include the county and city or village. There are also townships within counties. Other local governments have special purposes and include school dis-

Bill Campbell

Dick Paulus

tricts and many other types, from library to airport districts. Before you tackle local governments, you first need to understand the relationship of powers between the national and state governments.

Federalism in the U.S. Constitution

The powers of the national government, in relation to the states, are outlined in the U.S. Constitution. Certain powers are "expressed," meaning they are directly mentioned in the Constitution. Most of the expressed powers of the national government are listed in the first three articles of the Constitution. Among the expressed powers are such things as making treaties, coining money, raising and maintaining an army, declaring war, and carrying on relations with foreign governments.

Another type of power is "implied" in the Constitution, meaning that these powers are necessary to govern but are not listed in the Constitution. In order to raise an army for example, the government has sometimes used a "draft," which requires eligible citizens to serve in the military. Although not specified in the Constitution, a draft was found necessary for raising an army in times of crisis. The U.S. Congress passed a bill establishing a draft, the president signed the bill into law, and the U.S. Supreme Court decided that the power was allowed by the U.S. Constitution. (All men, at age eighteen, must register with the U.S. Selective Service for a possible draft into military service.)

In order for the national government to do things that are necessary but not listed in the Constitution, it relies on Article 1, Section 8. It gives the national government the ability to "... make all Laws which shall be necessary and proper ..." to carry out its duties under the Constitution. Like a rubber band, this "elastic clause" allows government to expand or retract its authority.

One example of national authority occurred in the 1970s when an oil shortage threatened the nation. Congress, in an attempt to conserve oil, passed a fifty-five miles per hour speed limit law for the nation. At the time state highways generally had speed limits of sixty-five or seventy miles per hour. The Illinois General Assembly, like many other states' legislatures, did not feel the lower speed limit was necessary and refused to adopt it. In order to enforce the fifty-five miles per hour speed limit, Congress said federal money for state highways would not be sent to a state unless the state complied with the national speed limit. In need of such money to maintain highways, Illinois reluctantly accepted the limit imposed by Congress. In this case the ability of the national government to "dictate" to the states seemed necessary.

The framers of the U.S. Constitution were skeptical of the authority of the strong national government they were creating, and they placed certain limitations on it. In Article 1, Section 9, they specifically denied certain powers to the national government.

Still fearful that individual rights of citizens might be abused either by the national or state government, ten amendments were added soon after the adoption of the U.S. Constitution. They are called the Bill of Rights. Nine of the ten protect specific rights of citizens, and the Tenth Amendment protects the powers reserved to the states. The Tenth Amendment says: "The powers not delegated to the United States by the Constitution, nor prohibited by it to the States, are reserved to the States respectively, or to the people."

As a result, states can exercise any power not given to the national government nor denied to them by the Constitution. For example, Illinois can establish a public school system, regulate licenses for driving, and set age limits to purchase alcohol.

Terry Farmer / Showcase Photography

Chicago's O'Hare Field is known as the world's busiest airport. This is the American Airlines terminal at O'Hare. While the city operates the airport, federal laws and regulations govern the airlines because they are involved in interstate commerce.

Just as they were fearful of an overly powerful national government, the framers saw the need to restrict state authority as well. Article 1, Section 10 lists the powers denied to the states. Specifically, the states cannot make treaties, coin money, tax imports and exports, or declare war.

You can see that federalism works by defining both the authority and limitations of the national and state governments' powers. There is yet another set of powers in federalism: "Concurrent powers" are shared by the national and state governments, meaning they use them at the same time. A good example is the power to tax. In Illinois, citizens pay a federal cigarette tax, a state cigarette tax, and in some cases a city cigarette tax. Each level of government sets the amount of tax and decides how the tax money will be used. As long as a power is not specifically reserved to either the state or national government, it may be shared. The ability to share power is one of the most important aspects of federalism. By sharing certain powers, government at the different levels can each deal with a similar problem but in different ways. For example, smoking is a health hazard. The national government has banned smoking in airplanes it regulates. Illinois state government has passed laws assuring there is no smoking in most public buildings in the state. Both governments have acted to protect the health of citizens.

What happens if a conflict arises over which level of government has a certain power? Article VI, Section 2 of the U.S. Constitution states:

> This Constitution, and the Laws of the United States which shall be made in pursuance thereof; and all Treaties made, or which shall be made, under the Authority of the United States, shall be the supreme Law of the Land, and the Judges in every State shall be bound thereby, anything in the Constitution or Laws or any State to the Contrary notwithstanding.

This is the "supremacy clause" that restricts state laws and state constitutions from conflicting with the U.S. Constitution and laws. Since the U.S. Constitution and laws are supreme, state officials are expected to follow them. Local governments, such as cities and counties, which get their authority from the state, cannot pass laws conflicting with the U.S. Constitution and federal laws or with the state Constitution and state laws.

Rights and Responsibilities of the Federal System

The idea of shared power works only when both the national and state governments fulfill their responsibilities to each other. For example, the U.S. Constitution guarantees to each state a republican form of government. This means that the national government must give each state its fair representation in the U.S. Congress. It also means that the national government must assure the citizens in each state that their state government will be directed by persons who are elected by the voters of that state. If this sounds boring, consider people who live in some Eastern European countries

The State Journal-Register / Sangamon Valley Collection, Lincoln Library

While the General Assembly debated, hundreds of supporters and opponents of the Equal Rights Amendment to the U.S. Constitution rallied on the Illinois Capitol lawn in the spring and summer of 1981.

The State Journal-Register

The sale of fireworks is not allowed generally by Illinois statute, but local governments can authorize people or organizations to buy them by issuing permits. The Illinois General Assembly passed the laws to protect the public's safety, and the local governments issuing permits have the responsibility of assuring the public that the fireworks will be used in a safe manner by anyone who gets a permit. Railroads, public utilities, and transportation carriers need permits even if they are using fireworks as signals or lighting. Only state and county fair associations may use fireworks without permits.

who have been trying in 1990 and 1991 to re-establish their own governments controlled since World War II by the Soviet Union's central government.

The national government of our United States of America also has responsibility for protecting states against invasion and domestic violence. At times during our history, the national government has been asked to restore calm within a state. During railroad rioting in Chicago in 1877 and the early 1880s, for example, federal troops were called in to restore peace.

The national government must also respect the geographic boundaries of each state. Article IV, Section 3 of the U.S. Constitution clearly explains that "... no new State shall be formed or erected within the Jurisdiction of any other State ... without the Consent of the Legislatures ...."

Beyond the expectation to cooperate with the national government, states also have specific responsibilities. All elections for national government officials—the president, the vice president, U.S. senators and U.S. representatives — are carried out by the states. The dates for the national general elections are set by national law, but the state sets the hours, place, and manner in which all elections are carried out.

Understanding that the U.S. Constitution might need to be altered by future events, the framers allowed for a method of amendment. The states play an important part in the amending process. No amendment to the U.S. Constitution can take effect unless three-fourths of the states approve it. While a single state's acceptance or rejection of a proposed amendment would seem relatively minor among actions of all fifty states, it can be of great importance. An example is the proposed Equal Rights Amendment (guaranteeing women and men equal rights as citizens) which was submitted to the states for ratification about twenty years ago. By 1977, only thirty-five of a necessary thirty-seven states had approved the proposed amendment, and it failed to become part of the U.S. Constitution. Illinois, whose Constitution grants equal protection of individual rights to men and women in its own Bill of Rights, was one of the states that did not ratify the amendment.

At the time, most political analysts felt that if Illinois were to ratify the amendment, other states would follow. In Illinois, the Equal Rights Amendment did not get enough votes to pass in the Illinois General Assembly. For Illinois to ratify an amendment, both the Illinois House and Illinois Senate must approve it.

The most recent example of the states' power to change the U.S. Constitution took place in July 1971, when the Twenty-Sixth Amendment gave eighteen-year-olds the right to vote. Prior to this amendment most states, including Illinois, required citizens to be at least twenty-one years of age to be qualified to vote. Pressure came for the change from citizens. The national government was sending U.S. military forces to fight in Vietnam, and the argument was that if military service began at age eighteen, so should the right to vote. In 1970, Congress lowered the voting age, but the U.S. Supreme Court ruled that Congress did not have the power to set voting age qualifications for elections, that it was a state power according to the U.S. Constitution. Congress has the power to propose constitutional amendments, so it proposed one to give all eighteen-year-olds the right to vote. The required number of states quickly ratified it, including Illinois — by votes in the General Assembly. The amendment process is one reason the Constitution is known as a "living document."

Photos by Bud Roberts / Illinois Army National Guard

The Illinois Army and Air National Guard provide help in case of emergencies in the state, if the governor orders them to help. Within Illinois state government, the Illinois Army and Air National Guard is called the Department of Military Affairs, which reports to the governor. This picture shows Illinois army guardsmen training for a medical evacuation.

The Illinois Army and Air National Guard can be ordered by the president to help regular U.S. military forces. An Illinois guardsman guides a truck onto a railcar for transportation to Saudi Arabia in 1990 to supply U.S. troops in Operation Desert Shield, which became Desert Storm when U.S. and allied forces fought Iraqi forces in Kuwait.

Relations between the States

While the basis for our U.S. Constitution is the cooperation between the states and the national government, relations between and among the states are also important. They must cooperate with and respect one another. States did not cooperate under the old Articles of Confederation. Contracts or legal notices made in one state were ignored in another. Extradition of criminals from one state to another was not guaranteed nor generally accepted. State borders, especially those along rivers, were a constant source of conflict. States were generally jealous or envious of others. The people in the small states with less land and smaller populations felt threatened by large ones, and large states often ignored small states. Wealthy states were envied by poor states. Even states of comparable size and wealth were hostile to each other. Competition among the states was strong. It still is.

With such a background, the framers carefully approached the question of interstate relations. Their answer is in Article IV: Each state is to honor the actions of the other states, respecting court decisions, laws, and various licenses. Today, each state accepts most legal documents of the others. For example, a driver's license from Illinois allows the holder to drive legally when in other states.

Article IV also expects each state to give citizens of the other states the same rights as its own citizens. There are some exceptions allowed by the U.S. Supreme Court. For example, as an Illinois citizen you may attend a state-funded university, go to a state-owned park, or get a state fishing license. Someone from Indiana or Florida cannot be barred from any of those Illinois public places or from getting a state license, but as out-of-state residents they can be charged more than Illinois residents.

Each state's law applies to anyone living in or visiting the state. Assume that selling fireworks is legal in Indiana. In Illinois, the state legislature has outlawed the sale of fireworks. An Illinois resident drives to Indiana and buys a trunkload of fireworks. Can he, as a resident of Illinois, legally buy these fireworks? Yes, because while in Indiana he was under Indiana law. What if the same individual brought the fireworks back to Illinois and sold them? Can he legally sell them in Illinois since they were bought legally in Indiana? No, because the Illinois law governs his actions when they take place in Illinois. The application of individual state laws within their own borders is a part of the respect idea of Article IV.

Extradition of criminals is another understanding between the states. If a person charged with a crime in Illinois flees to Michigan, he or she is supposed to be returned to Illinois by Michigan to stand trial under Illinois law. The U.S. Constitution gives each state's governor the responsibility for abiding by extradition agreements. The governor does have the option of refusing the extradition of someone to another state, but most states willingly cooperate with one another in criminal matters.

Illinois' State Constitution

While the U.S. Constitution is supreme in our nation, each state has its own constitution setting out the powers and organization of its state government. Before Illinois could become a state, it had to adopt a constitution. That was in 1818; since then, Illinois has adopted a new constitution three times. The present Illinois Constitution was drafted in a constitutional convention held in 1969 and 1970 and ratified by the state's voters in December 1970.

Illinois' Constitution is much like the U.S. Constitution. It contains a bill of rights and separate articles which provide for a legislative branch (called the Illinois General Assembly), an executive branch (headed by the governor as the state's chief executive officer), and a judicial branch with three levels of state courts (headed by the Illinois Supreme Court). The Illinois Constitution also establishes the state's local government and public education systems.

Most government services are, in fact, delivered to citizens by the state government, not by the national government. It is state government that has the primary responsibility for education, public safety, health and welfare, and the regulation of business and the professions. While it is true that the national government may pass laws and provide money for all these services, it is the state government that delivers these services to its citizens, in some programs according to federal guidelines which define how the services are to be delivered. It is also state government that figures out how to get much of the money to finance the services that citizens expect.

Education Is State Responsibility

Education is one such area of state responsibility. It is different in other nations. In some Western European countries, students in a particular grade study the same subject matter at the same time, throughout the entire country. Requirements for graduation are exactly the same in every school of the nation: To receive a diploma, students must pass a standardized test. Unlike these nations, the United States does not have a national policy for education. In fact, the U.S. Constitution does not deal with education at all.

Article X of Illinois' Constitution establishes responsibility for education. Section 1 says:

> A fundamental goal of the People of the State is the educational development of all persons to the limits of their capacities.
>
> The State shall provide for an efficient system of high quality public educational institutions and services. Education in public schools through the secondary level shall be free. There may be such other free education as the General Assembly provides by law.
>
> The State has the primary responsibility for financing the system of public education.

In order to oversee the state's educational system the Illinois Constitution created a State Board of Education. The board is responsible for establishing general goals, evaluating programs, and suggesting ways to finance schools.

Education is a good example of how the federalism concept of shared responsibility extends through the state to the local level. The actual responsibility for education has been passed on, by the state, to local school districts. In 1990, Illinois had 954 public school districts. While the state legislature passes laws affecting all the districts and the State Board of Education does much planning, each local district elects a board to set local school policy and control the budget. There are exceptions, notably Chicago, where school board members are appointed by the city government. Under school reform legislation enacted in 1989 by the General Assembly, however, every Chicago school (over 500 of them) elected a local school council to administer its school. There is still an overall Chicago Board of Education and a central administrative office run by a superintendent, but the school councils have been granted specific powers to control their own schools.

Despite the constitutional promise that the state has the primary responsibility for financing the system of public education, local property taxpayers in many school districts provide the majority of funds to operate their schools. Some districts are poorer than others, however. The result of this imbalance in funding results in a wide difference from district to district in the money spent to teach each student. Paying taxes for your education in Illinois is an issue today. If the state is to give more money to the less wealthy districts, it might have to increase taxes. But state taxes are paid by everyone in Illinois, and taxpayers in the wealthy districts might complain because their districts would not get any more money from the state. Money is often the issue in government. Few citizens want to pay more taxes, but at the same time many want government to spend more money on "good" things like education.

Public Safety Is Shared Responsibility

Public safety is another area of shared government authority. The U.S. Constitution gives Congress the power to maintain military forces to protect the nation. State government, in turn, is given the right to have a militia (called a national guard) to keep peace and enforce its laws. The national guard is seldom used except in emergencies. The guard may be called out if there is a bad flood or earthquake damage; it may be called out to control riots, such as during the 1968 Democratic National Convention in Chicago. It may also be called into active service by the president as part of the national armed services as in Operation Desert Shield and Desert Storm in the Persian Gulf.

In the Preamble of its Constitution, Illinois government is given the responsibility of providing for the "safety and welfare" of the people. The state government's direct response to this duty is a rather limited one. The Illinois State Police have only about 2,000 officers patrolling the highways, investigating certain violations of the law, and providing protection for state officials. In addition, the State Police provide assistance to local authorities through the state crime lab and other specialized services.

As in education, the majority of police are under the control of local governments. Each of the 102 counties in the state has a sheriff's department. Within those counties nearly 1,300 cities, villages, and towns have police departments ranging in size from Chicago with hundreds of officers to small towns with only one. Every level of government shares the responsibility for the safety of citizens.

Terry Farmer / Showcase Photography

In Illinois, almost every city has a police department, and every county has a sheriff's department. The largest city police force is in Chicago, but the State Police provide the patrolling of the interstate highways in the city and its metropolitan area. This picture shows Chicago policemen with some children in front of Buckingham Fountain in Grant Park next to Lake Michigan.

Illinois State Police *Illinois State Police*

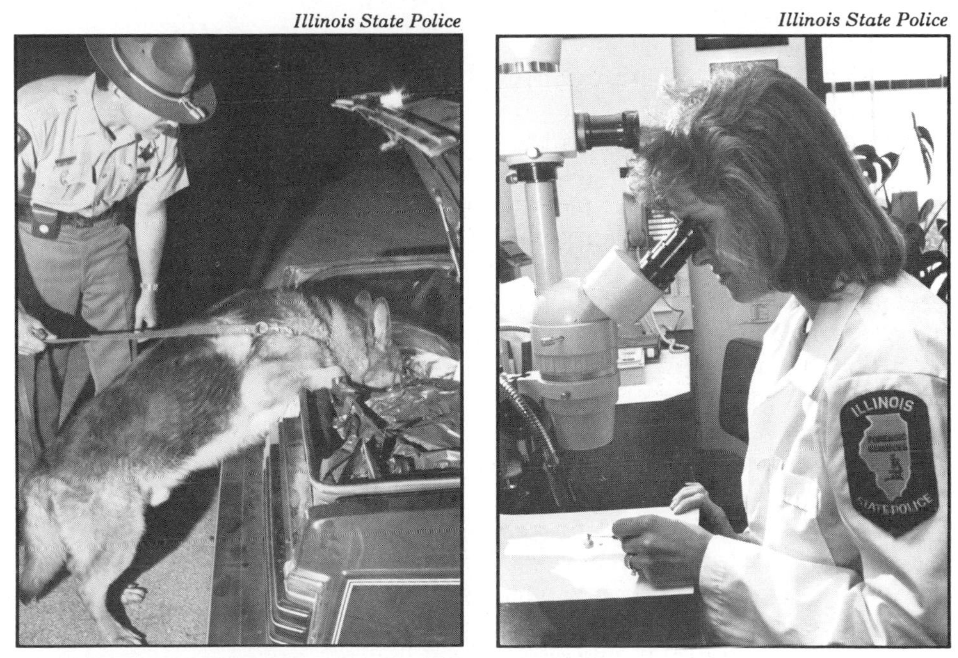

The Illinois State Police do more than patrol the highways. At left is a state trooper and his canine partner searching for drugs in the trunk of a car. At right is an Illinois State Police forensic scientist examining paint evidence through a stereo microscope in a State Police lab.

Health and Welfare Responsibilities

A third area where the state expands on the national government's responsibility is in health and welfare. Illinois has state agencies to inspect food, monitor diseases, and license physicians and nurses. The mentally ill are treated in state hospitals or provided care in their communities with state financial support. State agencies provide services for families and children, specifically protecting children from child abuse and granting to poorer citizens both welfare payments and health services. Other state departments assist in helping people with alcohol and drug problems and in rehabilitation of disabled people.

The growing national concern over the environment is also a state and local issue. The Illinois Constitution establishes that providing and maintaining a healthful environment is the public policy of the state and the duty of each person. The Illinois Environmental Protection Agency and the Illinois Pollution Control Board see that state environmental laws are obeyed. Air and water quality, radiation control, garbage and sewage disposal, and hazardous waste management are only a few of the areas regulated by state laws. There are also federal environmental laws which the state and its residents must obey.

As might be expected when responsibility is shared, there are disagreements between governments. When the national government recently approached the state for permission to deposit hazardous solid waste material in abandoned mines in southern and central Illinois, the Illinois legislature gave tentative approval. Several possible sites were selected. Then as more information was released on the type and hazards of the waste material, many citizens did not like the idea and the state reconsidered. It rejected the proposal. This is a good example of how state government can exercise its rights over the national government.

Business Regulation by Government

Regulation of business has also fallen onto the shoulders of state governments. The U.S. Constitution

Illinois Environmental Protection Agency

The wastewater from Illinois homes and businesses is cleaned and treated at more than 2,600 municipal and industrial wastewater treatment facilities regulated by the Illinois Environmental Protection Agency. The digesters shown in the picture are one method of treating water so the water will not pollute rivers and streams.

Illinois Environmental Protection Agency

Scrap tires have become not only an environmental concern but also a health concern. Disease-carrying mosquitoes are attracted to the water that collects in the tires. The Illinois Environmental Protection Agency regulates the number of tires stored. State agencies are exploring ways to recycle scrap tires into road and building materials.

IllinoisEnvironmental Protection Agency

The federal Clean Air Act of 1990 requires industries to make changes at their facilities to control air pollution. The Illinois Environmental Protection Agency regulates the Clean Air Act in Illinois.

Terry Farmer / Showcase Photography

Chemicals used on farms are also an environmental concern. Many farmers' tillage practices promote erosion caused by run-off from rain. Rain may transport soil and chemicals from the farmer's fields into ponds, lakes, streams, and rivers. The chemicals then become pollutants endangering the public's health, water supplies, and aquatic ecosystems rather than a help to farmers in producing abundant crops. The Illinois Environmental Protection Agency monitors groundwater pollution.

gave Congress the power to regulate commerce among the states. This so-called "commerce clause" of the Constitution has been used by Congress to regulate television and radio stations, airlines, railroads, and other companies doing business in different states. But, for the most part, businesses operating within the borders of Illinois are regulated by state laws.

Public utility companies such as Commonwealth Edison, Northern Illinois Gas, or Illinois Power are subject to the regulations imposed by state law. Insurance companies, real estate agencies, and even funeral homes are governed by rules established by the state. Working conditions are also affected by the state. The safety and sanitary conditions of our factories, as well as the number of hours an employee may work, are established by the state. The state oversees the unemployment insurance program for workers who lose their jobs in Illinois and the workers' compensation program for workers hurt on the job.

Local Government in Illinois

Yet another level of shared responsibility exists between Illinois state government and local governments within the state. The 102 county governments and the 2,000-plus city and village governments, however, are not partners with the state in the same sense as the state is with the national government. Local governments generally have only the powers granted them by state statutes, but there is an exception.

Article VII of the Illinois 1970 Constitution gives home rule to some local governments. Home rule means that local governments can, within limits, determine their own powers. To try something new, home rule local governments do not have to get a state law enacted like the rest of the local governments. According to Article VII, all cities and villages with populations over 25,000 have home rule. If a smaller city or village wants home rule, it can gain home rule status if its voters approve by referendum. Voters can also take away home rule by referendum. About 100 Illinois cities and villages have home rule.

County governments can also have home rule, but the power and structure of the county government is the qualification, not population. Only Cook County, the most populous, has had home rule since the 1970 Illinois Constitution was adopted.

No other type of local government in Illinois can have home rule. So most of Illinois' counties, cities and villages and all of its townships, school districts, airport authorities, library districts, and other local governments with special services depend on state laws for their powers.

Common to all Illinois local governments, which often overlap in their boundaries and in their services to

Terry Farmer / Showcase Photography

While most small businesses in the state are regulated by state government, there are federal regulations that affect business in Illinois. For example, every business must report salaries paid to employees to the U.S. Department of Revenue for the purpose of collecting federal and state income taxes.

Jon Randolph

Elgin is one of Illinois' home rule cities. Once famous as the city where "Elgin" watches were made, it is at the western edge of the booming Chicago metropolitan area's suburbs. With a 1990 population of 77,010, Elgin has older neighborhoods like the one in this picture as well as new subdivisions at its edges. A projected population growth of 20,000 over the next twenty years poses challenges for the city to provide services while trying to maintain its identity as a community.

Caterpillar Inc.

This aerial view shows the 600-acre site of Caterpillar Inc.'s Decatur plant. The main assembly building (just right of center) covers twenty-four acres, which is comparable to putting eighteen football fields under one roof. Altogether, the plant buildings cover a total of 3.1 million square feet. Close by this plant on Decatur's northeast side are two other corporations, A.E. Staley and Archer Daniels Midland. Farther east is the campus of Richland Community College. Local property taxes paid by the companies help support local government, including Decatur's schools and the community college.

the public, is that decisions are made by boards representing the citizens within the boundaries — and taxes are levied within the boundaries to fund the local government services.

Local government in Illinois finances itself, much like the state and nation, by taxing its residents. Unlike the state and nation which tax income, local governments in Illinois tax property. Homeowners, farm owners, and business owners pay taxes on their residences, buildings, and lands. Property taxes account for well over half of the money available to local governments. But Illinois state government shares some of the state income tax money with all the counties, cities, and villages in Illinois. It gives other money to local governments, too, such as schools. The state also receives money from the national government, for example, to build major highways and fund welfare programs.

The different levels of government could not function without the concurrent ability to tax and spend money, independent from the other levels, but local governments depend on some money from the state government, and the state government depends on some money from the national government.

While some local governments have greater independence under home rule, they also have specific limitations on taxing powers set by the Illinois Constitution. A home rule government cannot pass a local income tax, unless the Illinois state legislature decides to give this authority to all the municipalities and counties in the state.

Bill Campbell

We the People

In the United States, our system of government has many levels, and the concept of federalism holds them together. The Preamble of the U.S. Constitution begins with the words, "We the people of the United States," and the Preamble of the Illinois Constitution begins, "We, the people of the State of Illinois." In both documents it is the people that government is meant to represent. Federalism, from the national through the state to the local level, allows the people a clear and direct voice in deciding their own affairs through their elected representatives. As you continue to study the state Constitution, remember that each level of government is a link in the chain that represents "We the People."

CHAPTER 4

The Legislative Game: How To Pass Your Law

By Judy Lee (Lewis) Uphoff

If you want a law passed in Illinois, there is only one way to do that: You must become a player in the legislative game. The game is played every year from the second Wednesday in January until the end of June in the Capitol in Springfield, Illinois. That's when the Illinois General Assembly is in session. The chief players are, of course, the 177 legislators elected by the people in their districts. These legislators are the members of the Illinois General Assembly, which forms the legislative branch of Illinois' state government. (See box, on page 44, "Electing 118 House Members, 59 Senate Members.")

The main duty or function of the legislative branch is to make or enact laws — or prevent the enactment of laws — for the people of the state. The legislative branch is divided into two houses — the House of Representatives and the Senate. Since Illinois patterned its government after the U.S. Constitution, having two houses in the legislative branch is essential. No bill can become a law unless it passes both houses of the legislative branch with exactly the same wording. This arrangement makes passing legislation more difficult than if there were only one chamber. This was exactly the idea: To protect the people of the state from useless or even dangerous legislation, two houses must agree that the bill should become a law.

Bill Campbell

All of the above may sound a little complicated, and you may think that, just because you are only a student and not a legislator, there is no way for you to play or even have any part in the legislative game. However, you, too, can play the game with a chance of passing the legislation that you wish to see enacted.

The basic rules are fairly easy, but as in most games it often takes more than just knowing the rules to win — it takes strategy, too.

Legislators can easily learn the basic rules of how a bill becomes a law, but they will not get bills enacted if they use the wrong strategy. Sometimes there are difficult decisions that make the game very hard to play — and win. Legislators must often make deals with other legislators to get support for their bills. Some bills may favor one part of the state over another, becoming a Chicago-versus-downstate issue. Others might be good for the environment but cost businesses extra money. Sometimes legislators must decide between

> **Getting a Bill Passed To Become a Law**
>
> See Section 8 of Article IV of the Illinois Constitution for how a bill becomes law. Key steps for a bill are Introduction, First Reading, Assigned to a Committee, Committee Hearings, Committee Vote. If passed by committee, a bill goes to Second Reading where Amendments and Votes on Amendments are crucial. If it passes on Second Reading, it goes to Third Reading where there is Debate and a Roll Call Vote. If it passes the Third Reading vote, it goes to the other chamber of the General Assembly, where it will follow all of the same steps. See the chart on page 46 for every detail in the process, including the governor's action. The most direct way for a bill to become law after it is passed by both the House and Senate is for the governor to sign it.

The State Journal-Register

Joint sessions of the Illinois General Assembly take place in the House of Representatives' chamber because it is larger than the Senate chamber in the Capitol in Springfield. Former Gov. James R. Thompson is at the podium delivering his 1989 State of the State address to all the legislators. Circling the chamber are galleries where visitors are welcome to listen and watch. Usually, only the legislators and their staffs are allowed on the floor of the chamber.

what they personally believe and what their constituents (people in their own districts) feel is important. They sometimes must decide between loyalty to their political party leaders and what they think is best.

The Players and Object of the Game

But let's get on with the game so you will understand how it works. To play the game you must pick the playing piece you wish to use. You have four choices: Citizen, Lobbyist, Party Leader, and Governor. The object of the game is to convince the General Assembly to pass your bill. This is a complicated game involving a process that gives each legislator a vote and requires a majority vote to move a bill forward at each step.

A citizen is anyone living in Illinois who thinks that some state law needs to be passed or changed. A citizen may be any age and have any kind of background. Usually he or she has found other citizens who believe that the same law needs to be passed or changed.

A lobbyist is a person who is hired by some group to get bills passed or defeated. Many of your parents may belong to groups that lobby. There are labor unions such as the UAW (United Auto Workers) and IEA (Illinois Education Association); professional and business organizations such as the AMA (American Medical Association), Illinois State Chamber of Commerce, Illinois Realtors, and the Farm Bureau; and other special interest organizations such as the NRA (National Rifle Association) and the Citizens for a Better Environment. These and many other groups hire lobbyists to influence legislators to vote for bills that would be beneficial to their group — or to vote against bills that would hurt their interests.

Party leaders are influential members of the Democratic or Republican parties. They also try to decide what bills need to be passed. They encourage the legislators who belong to their party to introduce and pass bills that they feel are important. They also try to get individual legislators from their party to take positions on issues that will help the party win the next election.

The governor and other top government leaders such as the secretary of state, attorney general, directors of state agencies, and the governor's aides also try to get legislation passed that they feel is important. They often try to influence legislators by the power of their position, but they can only suggest legislation; they cannot introduce bills.

On with the Game: The Citizen Player

To get on with our game, I am going to assume that you have chosen to be yourself—a citizen. On our game board (see pages 36 and 37), you will see two places to start: the path through the House and the path through the Senate. But, read the fine print: Only a representative can proceed down the House path, and only a senator can proceed down the Senate path. You cannot directly vote in this process; only the representatives and senators have that power. You cannot introduce a bill directly onto the board; only a representative or a senator may do so.

Think of it as if it were a tag-team sporting event. For the citizen, lobbyist, governor, or party leader to get legislation passed, they must "tag" a legislator to introduce and sponsor a bill for them. To tag a legislator in this game means that you must convince the legislator that your legislation is worthwhile — that something really needs to be changed in Illinois.

Getting a Legislator To Sponsor Your Bill

Although you can suggest any legislation that you would like, let's assume that the bill you would like to see passed into law is one that would allow fourteen-year-olds to get their driver's licenses. You must convince either your senator or your representative that this legislation is worthwhile. You only need to convince one of them to introduce your legislation, but before it can become a law, it will have to be passed by both houses of the General Assembly. (See box, "Getting a Bill Passed To Become Law.") That is why most players of the game try to get at least one sponsor for their bill in the House and at least one sponsor in the Senate.

How can you convince a representative or a senator to introduce this legislation? First, prepare your facts. Why is this legislation needed? I'm sure you can think of several reasons that you might suggest to your representative. You may write a letter, telephone, or try

Party and Legislative Leadership

The term "party leadership" in the General Assembly includes the leaders of both the Democrats and Republicans in both the Senate and the House. That means four top party leaders in the legislature. There are also very influential party leaders outside the General Assembly who can influence legislators. The governor is one. Another is the mayor of Chicago.

Which party has more power? The one with a majority of members, obviously, because it can approve bills. But one party may be the majority in the House, and the other may have the majority in the Senate. Whichever party has less than a majority of members is called the minority party. Both the House and Senate have minority leaders.

The majority leader in the Senate is the Senate president. The majority leader in the House is a separate position almost always held by a representative of the same party as the speaker of the House. The Senate president presides over meetings of the Senate, and the speaker of the House presides over those meetings of the House. They decide when bills will come up for debate and vote in their respective chambers. While the House speaker may not be officially called the majority leader, the speaker is considered by most to be the leader of his party's members in the House.

The leaders are very powerful in the Illinois General Assembly. As the leaders of their parties, they help members of their party get elected to office, appoint them to committees and leadership positions in the legislature, hire partisan staff, and direct their party's work in legislative sessions. They can and do have a strong influence on how individual members of the General Assembly vote on bills.

Many people feel that all of the important decisions in the General Assembly are really made by the five principal political leaders: the governor, the president of the Senate, the Senate minority leader, the speaker of the House, and the House minority leader. In truth, these five officers frequently do meet to try to reach an agreement on what a bill must provide to be acceptable to each of them and their political parties. When they reach an agreement on a bill, they then try, usually successfully, to get enough votes from the other members of the General Assembly to pass and enact the bill into law.

Local political party leaders, such as the mayor of Chicago and Democratic or Republican party chairman in each county, also have a strong influence over the votes of those members of the General Assembly who represent their county or city. This is because these local leaders, through their control over the local party's organization and money, can have a great deal of influence over party nominations and campaigns for election to seats in the General Assembly.

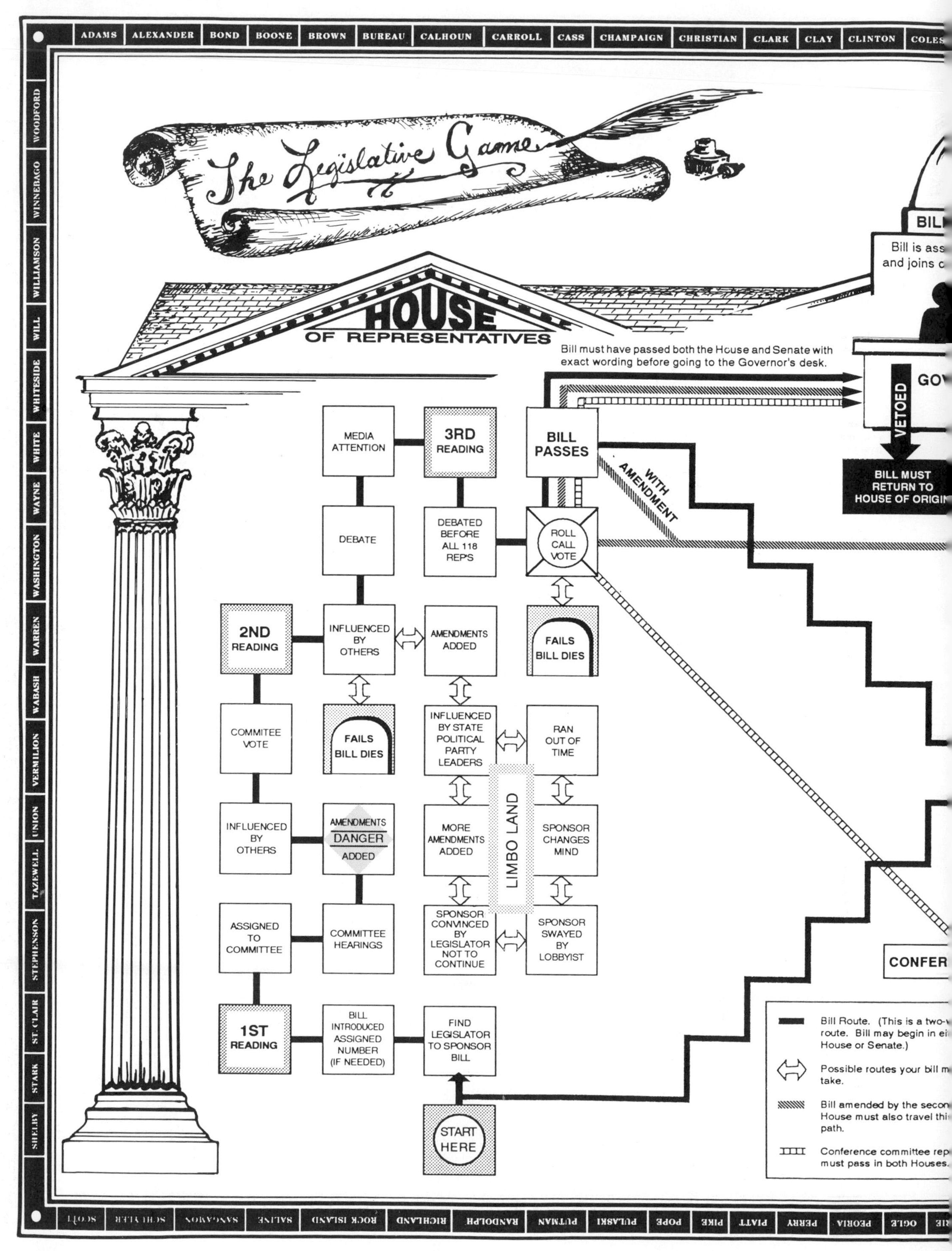
ADAMS
ALEXANDER
BOND
BOONE
BROWN
BUREAU
CALHOUN
CARROLL
CASS
CHAMPAIGN
CHRISTIAN
CLARK
CLAY
CLINTON
WOODFORD
WINNEBAGO
WILLIAMSON
WILL
WHITESIDE
WHITE
WAYNE
WASHINGTON
WARREN
WABASH
VERMILION
UNION
TAZEWELL
STEPHENSON
ST. CLAIR
STARK
SHELBY
SANGAMON
SALINE
ROCK ISLAND
RICHLAND
RANDOLPH
PUTNAM
PULASKI
POPE
PIKE
PIATT
PERRY
PEORIA
OGLE
The Legislative Game
HOUSE
OF REPRESENTATIVES
Bill is ass
and joins c
Bill must have passed both the House and Senate with exact wording before going to the Governor's desk.
VETOED
BILL MUST RETURN TO HOUSE OF ORIGI
MEDIA ATTENTION
3RD READING
BILL PASSES
WITH AMENDMENT
DEBATE
DEBATED BEFORE ALL 118 REP'S
ROLL CALL VOTE
2ND READING
INFLUENCED BY OTHERS
AMENDMENTS ADDED
FAILS BILL DIES
COMMITEE VOTE
FAILS BILL DIES
INFLUENCED BY STATE POLITICAL PARTY LEADERS
RAN OUT OF TIME
LIMBO LAND
INFLUENCED BY OTHERS
AMENDMENTS DANGER ADDED
MORE AMENDMENTS ADDED
SPONSOR CHANGES MIND
ASSIGNED TO COMMITTEE
COMMITTEE HEARINGS
SPONSOR CONVINCED BY LEGISLATOR NOT TO CONTINUE
SPONSOR SWAYED BY LOBBYIST
CONFER
1ST READING
BILL INTRODUCED ASSIGNED NUMBER (IF NEEDED)
FIND LEGISLATOR TO SPONSOR BILL
START HERE
Bill Route. (This is a two-w route. Bill may begin in ei House or Senate.)
Possible routes your bill m take.
Bill amended by the secon House must also travel thi path.
Conference committee rep must pass in both Houses.

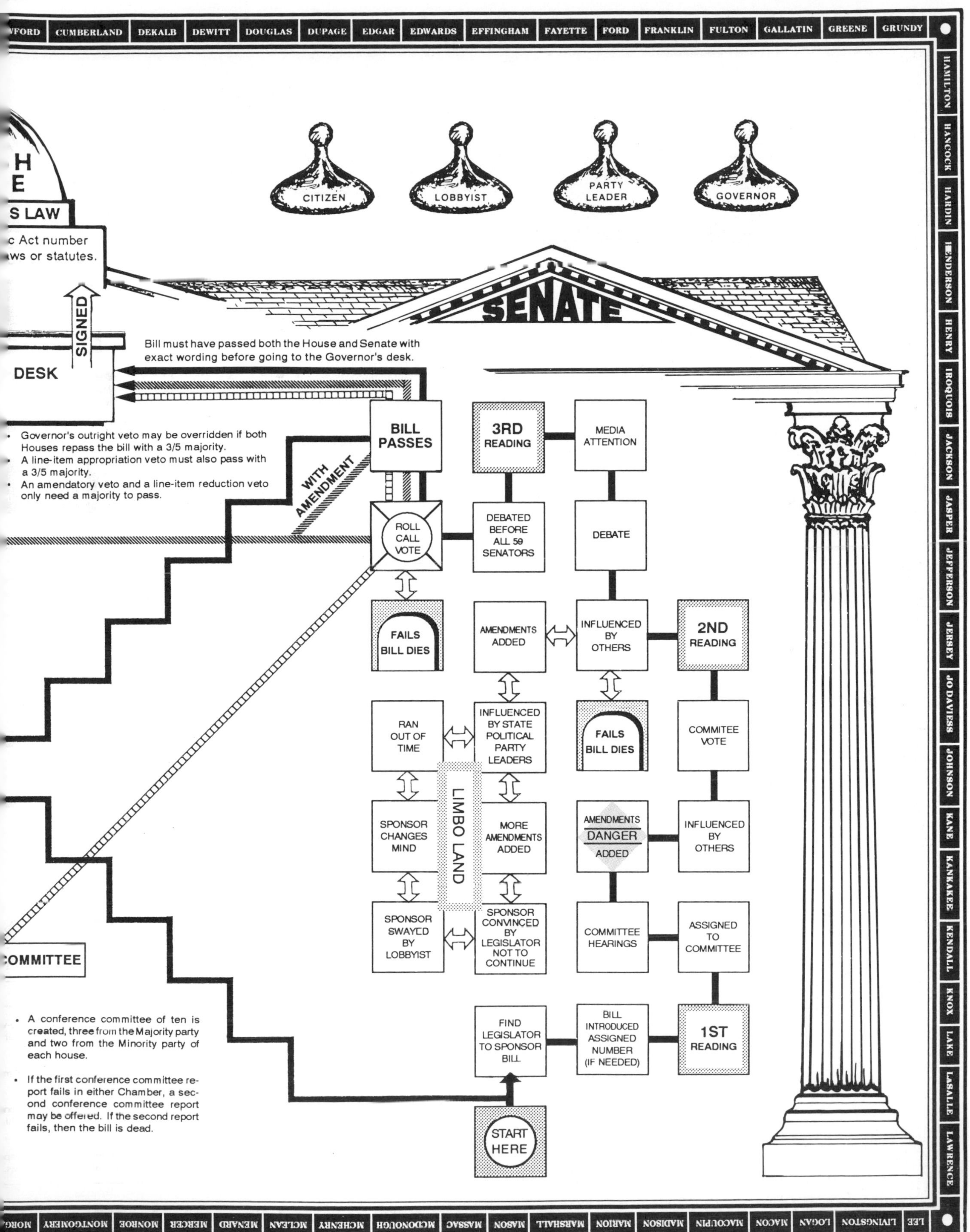

- Governor's outright veto may be overridden if both Houses repass the bill with a 3/5 majority.
- A line-item appropriation veto must also pass with a 3/5 majority.
- An amendatory veto and a line-item reduction veto only need a majority to pass.

- A conference committee of ten is created, three from the Majority party and two from the Minority party of each house.
- If the first conference committee report fails in either Chamber, a second conference committee report may be offered. If the second report fails, then the bill is dead.

Terry Farmer / Showcase Photography

These are the leaders of the Illinois General Assembly in early 1991. The Democrats, who had the majority of members in both the Senate and House, elected the House speaker and the Senate president. From left are Senate Minority Leader James "Pate" Philip, Speaker of the House Michael J. Madigan, House Minority Leader Lee A. Daniels, and Senate President Philip J. Rock.

to set up an appointment to meet with him or her personally. They have offices in their districts where you can reach them when they are not in Springfield. Let's assume that you are very convincing and that your representative chooses to introduce the legislation for you. He or she will have thought it through carefully before doing so.

Your representative would have to consider many things: how he or she feels personally about fourteen-year-olds driving, how the voters in his or her district will feel about fourteen-year-old drivers, and how different groups of people such as law enforcement groups, insurance groups, car dealers, and teachers will feel about the legislation. But remember that you are a very important person; not only are you a citizen, but also you go by another title — constituent. Your representative was elected to look out for the interests of the constituents in his or her district; these constituents are simply the people who live in the legislator's district. The constituents who are old enough to vote (and registered to vote) can reelect him or her — or vote for someone else to represent them at the next election.

Introducing Your Bill

You succeed in tagging your representative that your idea is a good one. Your representative introduces your legislation as a bill. By introducing your legislation in the House, your representative puts your bill on the game board at Bill Introductions. What about the other side of the game board? Eventually the Senate must also deal with your legislation if it is to become a law. In a recent — and typical — legislative session, over 6,500 bills were introduced, and only about 1,650 made it through both houses.

The first steps forward are easy to accomplish. The bill (or proposed law) is assigned a number. The number will begin with the letters "H.B." (the abbreviation for House Bill) since it is originating in the House of Representatives. The bill is placed on the "calendar" for future consideration. It is then read for the first time — called "First Reading." So far, your bill is progressing nicely, moving forward on the game board several squares.

Rocky Road of Committee Hearings

Now comes a crucial test — one that could kill your bill. All legislation must take this rocky road known as committee hearings. Most of the study and investigation of bills takes place in committee hearings. Each bill will be assigned to a committee to be studied. The committee to which it is assigned is usually based upon the content of the bill, but sometimes bills are assigned to certain committees for political reasons. Let's assume your bill was assigned to the appropriate committee — the House Committee on Transportation and Motor Vehicles.

The committee then begins the process of studying the bill. The committee must be convinced that the bill is good, or it will kill your bill at this point and the game will be over. The committee members will hear testimony from groups who will be affected by the bill. (See box, "Legislative Committees' Role in Passing a Bill.")

Try to think of people who would care whether fourteen-year-olds could legally drive, and you will be able to name some of the groups who might give testimony at committee hearings. Some of the people might be insurance company representatives, police officers, car dealers, school officials, and fourteen-year-olds. Lobbyists and the governor's staff will be busy at this point, too, letting the legislators know whether they support the bill. The key legislators at the committee

Jim Rogers / House Democratic Staff

Speaking on the House floor during debate is Rep. Larry Hicks, Democrat from Mount Vernon. Any one of the 118 representatives or fifty-nine senators can sponsor a bill in the General Assembly.

level are the Senate and House leaders. Think about why each of these groups might want to be represented at the committee hearings. Remember that this is one of the more dangerous sections on the game board, and it often takes cunning and political skill to get past this step.

Second Reading and the Clock Is Ticking

Let's assume that your bill makes it out of committee. Your legislator now must tackle the rest of the course to get this legislation passed — and the clock is ticking. A legislative session begins in January and ends in June. That may sound like a long time, but it actually is often not enough time to get many of the bills through the game board.

On the board your bill — with its legislative sponsor — has now come to a spot marked Second Reading. No bill may become a law unless it has made it through three readings. Can you think of reasons why those rules were included in this game?

You probably guessed that one reason was so that legislation could not be hurriedly passed through the General Assembly. Three readings give the bill a chance to be considered several times before the final vote is taken. Bills used to be read aloud in complete detail on three different days, but today each is read by number and a copy is printed and distributed.

Notice that one path your bill may take at second reading just drifts off into nowhere. Some bills are just ignored — neither passed nor killed, but in limbo. There are several reasons: The legislature may run out of time; the bill's sponsor may decide that there is too much opposition to the bill; another person or lobbyist may convince the sponsor to forget the bill; or the legislative leadership might convince the sponsor not to push for further action on the bill.

Beware of the Amendment Loop

If the bill gets further consideration on second reading, there may be amendments proposed which could change your bill — amendments that you may or may not agree should be added. Can you think of any amendments that you would not want tacked on? What if someone added a phrase that said only straight-A students could drive at age fourteen? Or what if, to get the needed votes to pass the bill, your legislator had to accept an amendment to the bill that said, "if a student drops out of school he or she automatically loses his or her license"?

Here is where some of those difficult decisions must

Bill Campbell

Legislative Committees' Role in Passing a Bill

Both the House and Senate have over a dozen committees made up of legislators. Every bill is sent first to a special committee whose job is to assign each bill to the appropriate committee for study. For example, a bill to build roads would go to the Transportation Committee. The chairman of the Transportation Committee will arrange for hearings on the bill with the legislator who sponsored the bill. Hearings are study meetings to which anyone can come and present arguments for or against the bill. Finding out among the committee members who does and does not support a bill is key to preparing arguments at this stage.

After the committee studies the bill, it votes to make one of the following recommendations: do pass, do pass as amended, do not pass, or do not pass as amended. If the committee recommends a "do not pass," the bill is considered dead. A sponsor of a bill may appeal to all the members of his or her house to revive the bill, but this rarely happens.

Dick Paulus

be made. What if your sponsor knew that his or her constituents would not want that "dropout" amendment? Some might feel it was unconstitutional to connect driving privileges with staying in school. Others might feel that problem students would just stay in school to keep their licenses but would disrupt their classes. Other students just might want to drop out and still drive. What if your representative allows this amendment to be added? Will a lot of the people in your district be angry at your representative? Will they be angry enough to vote for someone else? What if your representative doesn't allow this amendment and the bill never gets passed? What if your representative personally likes the amendment, but knows his or her constituents don't? This is when the game gets very difficult to play, and sometimes a legislator cannot satisfy all the people he or she wants to please.

The Power of Legislative Leaders

Often, too, the governor and the legislative leadership will become very active at this second reading stage, trying to get amendments passed to the bill which will change it more to their liking. The legislative leadership may be willing to help your sponsor get this bill passed, or it may try to get your sponsor to let the bill die. The legislative leaders have very great power over what bills get passed. You might want to try to meet with some of the legislative leaders to try to convince them to support your bill. That is often a very sound part of strategy in this game. (See box, "Party and Legislative Leadership.")

Kevin Jones / Senate Democratic Staff

Senate Assistant Majority Leader Earlean Collins (Democrat from Chicago) is at the podium, presiding over the session.

Remember that amendments must be voted on and must receive a majority vote of the members voting before they are included as part of the bill. Sometimes so many amendments get added to a bill that the person who suggested the original bill hardly recognizes it as the same one that was introduced. That's another reason why sponsors sometimes let their bills die.

The Pressures at Third Reading

Let's again assume that you are lucky at second reading. Your legislator is able to keep your bill on the straight path — without any really crucial amendments being added. You are now racing toward the finish line. Remember that there are over 6,000 bills considered each session and that each step on the game board often

Third Reading and Roll Call Votes

Bills cannot be amended at the Third Reading stage, and a roll call vote is required to pass third reading. The sponsor of the bill explains the bill on the floor with all members in the chamber and briefly describes its purpose. Each member is allowed five minutes to debate or question this bill (more specific rules concern this). All bills require a constitutional majority to pass (thirty votes in the Senate and sixty votes in the House). A roll call vote means every legislator's vote — yes, no, present, or absent — is recorded by name in the official record, called House Daily Journals and Senate Daily Journals. A transcript of all floor debate and proceedings is prepared and kept for each chamber by the secretary of the Senate and by the clerk of the House. These are published and your library can find them for you.

takes a good deal of time. You are now approaching the final hurdle (or at least it seems that way to you) — the Third Reading.

Up until this point your bill has been debated in committee, and it may have been debated if amendments were suggested, but now all 118 representatives have their turn to debate the bill before a final vote is taken. (See box, "Third Reading and Roll Call Votes.") Some bills go through third reading easily; some don't. I'm guessing your bill would cause heated debate. Some legislators would feel that it would be good to allow fourteen-year-olds to drive, and others would feel that it would be a horrible mistake. Try to argue from both sides because to convince any opponents to change their minds, you must first understand their arguments.

At this point the legislator is faced with a major question for which there is no written rule. Should a legislator vote how he or she personally feels about the issue, or should he or she vote the way their constituents want them to vote? What if a legislator thought that it would be great to let fourteen-year-olds drive, but that same legislator had received a lot of mail or phone calls from people in his or her district wanting him or her to vote "No." Which way should that legislator vote? Remember, there is no definite rule concerning what to do. Some legislators count the number of people from their district who tell them to vote "No" and the ones who tell them to vote "Yes," and then they vote the way the majority wants. Other legislators feel that they have more knowledge concerning the bill than their constituents and that they should vote what they believe is right. It is not an easy decision.

The news media will begin writing about proposed legislation as bills move through the process, especially when they come to third reading. Newspaper, television, and radio reports usually cause further reactions from citizens (including the representatives' constituents). At the same time the lobbyists will become very busy trying to get legislation passed or defeated, depending on how the particular group views each bill. The governor, legislative leaders, and party leaders will also use their influence again at this point to pass or defeat legislation.

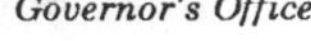

Governor's Office

State Superintendent of Education Robert Leininger is at left, meeting with Gov. Jim Edgar during the governor's first week in office in January 1991.

Sometimes a legislator is faced with a no-win situation. He or she will be pressured to do what the lobbyist or party leaders want instead of doing what the legislator thinks his or her constituents want.

Third Reading's Final Jeopardy

Following the debate comes the final jeopardy: All members of the House get to vote on your bill. All bills require a majority of the total membership to pass, and so you anxiously await the tally. It will take sixty "Yes"

Conference Committees

If the Senate and the House do not pass the bill in exactly the same form, the bill has not passed. Certain things can be done, however. If one chamber (or house) has added an amendment, it is sent to the other chamber for concurrence to the amendment. If one chamber refuses to drop the amendment and the other house refuses to add it, a conference committee is formed. This committee consists of five members from the House and five from the Senate who try to write a compromise version of the bill. The compromise is called a conference committee report on the bill, and it must be approved by a constitutional majority vote in both the House and Senate.

Veto Sessions

Because most of the bills finally passed by the General Assembly don't finish this complicated process until the last days of the session at the end of June, the governor does not have time to review them — and either sign or veto them — before the General Assembly completes its work in Springfield and members go home for the summer. The governor has sixty days to decide whether to sign or veto a bill after the General Assembly sends it to the governor.

Then in the fall — either October or November — the General Assembly meets again for its "fall veto session" to reconsider bills the governor has vetoed. The General Assembly, however, is not limited in the fall to only voting on vetoed bills.

Jim Rogers / House Democratic Staff

Three Democratic legislators from Chicago are conferring during House debate. From left are Reps. William Shaw, Robert LeFlore, Jr., and Paul L. Williams.

votes to pass your bill in the House. When the count is taken, sixty-two representatives have voted "Yes." Your bill has passed. So you think you've won the game? No, you have now advanced to the next level. Your bill now goes automatically to the Senate, and it must go through the exact same process again.

Game Level 2: Crossing over to the Senate

If your bill fails anywhere along the Senate path, it will be killed even though it was so successful in the House. If your House bill gets amended in the Senate and then is passed by a majority of senators at third reading, your House bill with its Senate amendment must be re-passed in the House. Remember the rules require that both houses pass identical bills. The House and Senate follow the same basic procedure in passing bills, but each also has precise rules.

Sometimes when the two houses pass a similar bill, but not the exact same bill, a conference committee is formed. If successful in ironing out differences, the conference committee reports a new version of the bill, which both chambers must approve. (See box, "Conference Committees.")

Vetoed Bills Must Start Over Again

Jay Barnard / Senate Republican Staff

The top Republican legislative leaders confer. At left is Senate Minority Leader James "Pate" Philip and House Minority Leader Lee A. Daniels.

Let's assume that your luck, and now skill, gets this bill through both the House and the Senate in exactly the same form. You still have not won the game. Before a bill becomes a law, it must not only pass both chambers of the General Assembly, but it must also be signed by the governor. If the governor does not like this bill, the governor may veto it. (Details on the governor's veto powers are in the next chapter.)

If your bill is vetoed by the governor, you still have one last chance to get your bill made into law. This time, however, both houses must re-pass your bill with a three-fifths vote. Those are the rules. In the House you would need 71 votes, and in the Senate 36 votes. Why do you suppose the Illinois Constitution was written to require more votes to re-pass a vetoed bill? Why would the Constitution allow the representatives and senators to pass a bill into law without the governor's approval?

Governor Approves Your Bill: It Becomes Law

In the actual process, it is more likely that the governor will approve your bill than veto it. So, you win! And the game is over. With the governor's signature on the bill, it becomes law. Officially it gets a Public Act number and joins all other Illinois laws, sometimes

Dick Paulus — *Bill Campbell* — *Dick Paulus*

called statutes. You are a hero or heroine to every fourteen-year-old in the state of Illinois! No more walking to school or begging rides from older brothers or sisters. Wow! All fourteen-year-olds start dreaming of passing the state driver's test.

Wait a minute. Some reporter just called you up and said a lot of fourteen-year-olds were complaining because their older brothers and sisters did not want to share their cars, and a lot of parents were calling to complain that they just found out car insurance for fourteen-year-olds costs too much. The reporter says one parent was so upset he might file a lawsuit challenging your new law in court.

Kevin Jones / Senate Democratic Staff

Senate President Philip J. Rock (at right) is presenting testimony at a Senate Appropriations Committee hearing in favor of the University of Illinois' request for funds. At left is University of Illinois President Stanley O. Ikenberry.

The Real Thing

Everything in this game is true, except for the bill idea we made up. It is hard to get a bill passed in the General Assembly, but the process is the best way to be certain that government works to balance what some people want against what others don't. But the legislative game is just one of the games that members of the Illinois General Assembly play. Another is the constituent game.

Jim Rogers / House Democratic Staff

House Speaker Michael J. Madigan is speaking to House members, not from the podium as speaker, but from his seat on the floor as a state representative.

The Constituent Game

In the constituent game, the object is to get reelected as a representative or senator. Each legislator is elected by the voters in his or her district. To get reelected to office, the legislator must earn the support of his or her constituents — the people who live in his or her district, especially those who vote.

Winning the support of constituents is not easy, especially when there are other people in the district who would like to serve in the legislature. Candidates win office because they appeal to their constituents — at least a majority — by their political party, their cultural background, their reputation, etc. If anyone else wants to win the district and serve in the General Assembly, they have to defeat the person who currently holds that office — the incumbent. Not every incumbent runs for reelection, but they do most of the time in Illinois. How does someone beat the incumbent? They will try to convince the voters in the district that the incumbent legislator is not doing a good job and that they can do better.

In most districts there are people who are critical of the bills passed by the legislature and of the members who voted for them. It is not easy to get people's support and loyalty in an atmosphere where free speech and critical thinking are generally encouraged. It is also not easy to defend a vote when people in the legislator's districts do not understand all the complexities of an issue or the intricate steps in the legislative process. But nobody said lawmaking was easy.

Keeping the Home District Happy

To win loyal support, legislators employ several strategies. One strategy you already know: They intro-

Bill Campbell

House Republican Staff

Senate Republican Staff

Many school groups visit Springfield every year to see the Capitol and other government buildings, including historic sites connected with Abraham Lincoln. If the General Assembly is in session, your state representative or senator will very likely arrange for a photograph like these. At left is a school group posed on the main staircase of the Capitol with Rep. Kathleen L. Wojcik, a Republican from Schaumburg. At right is another group, this time posed on the south steps of the Capitol with Sen. Laura Kent Donahue, a Republican from Quincy.

duce bills that their constituents want passed. But there are other strategies as well.

Perhaps the most important of these other strategies is helping their constituents. To win support, legislators provide all sorts of government help to the people in their districts. They will attempt to get state government to build or improve roads in their districts, to get new parks developed or new government buildings built. They will try to get state grants for local business and social service groups in their district.

Incumbents perform other services as well. Most legislators or their staffs spend much time helping their constituents in their dealings with state agencies. They may, for instance, help people to get jobs in state government, resolve problems involving welfare assistance, get appointments to meet with state officials, or gain admission to state hospitals or universities. They will help students find information for school assignments on state government. They will help your school make arrangements for a class trip to visit Springfield and the state Capitol. Through all these services, a legislator literally becomes his or her constituents'

Electing 118 House Members, 59 Senate Members

All information concerning the legislative branch can be found in Article IV of the Illinois Constitution. Section 2 in Article IV of the Constitution defines the makeup of the General Assembly. The state has to be redivided into fifty-nine legislative districts following the census every ten years. One senator is elected from each legislative district — thus fifty-nine Illinois senators. One-third of the districts have their senators chosen for a four-year term, a four-year term, and then a two-year term. One-third will serve a four-year term, a two-year term and a four-year term. The third group will serve a two-year term and then two four-year terms. This term setup works out so that every ten years all senators are up for reelection following the census and the redrawing of the districts. Each district is supposed to be equal in population.

Each legislative district that elects one senator is divided into two representative districts — thus 118 members in the House. One representative is elected from each district and serves a two-year term.

To be either a senator or a representative, you must be a U.S. citizen, twenty-one years old, and live in the district for two years prior to the election. You must also win the election in your district. Members are elected in even-numbered years. With the election in November, the House and Senate convene the following January. When they meet, the House of Representatives elects a speaker of the House, and the Senate elects a president of the Senate. The House and Senate also adopt detailed rules on how they will do their business.

Who They Are: State Legislators

Being a state legislator in Illinois takes a lot more time than it used to. Almost half of Illinois' 177 state legislators in 1989 listed their occupations as full-time senators or representatives. Twenty years ago, only five percent of them thought it was a full-time job.

Times have changed. The Illinois General Assembly now meets in Springfield every year both in the spring and in the fall. It becomes hard for many people to leave their business or take time off from their regular jobs to serve in the Illinois House or Senate.

The second biggest occupation that legislators list is attorneys-at-law. In 1989, there were thirty-four lawyers, which is about twenty percent of all General Assembly members.

In 1989, there were a half dozen farmers who were legislators, and around thirty legislators were in some type of business from insurance to banking, from printing to plumbing, from advertising to funeral homes.

representative in state government.

This Game's Prize: Winning Reelection

Interestingly, the more favors or services that legislators can provide for constituents, the better their chances of reelection. The more often legislators have been reelected, the more influence they are likely to have, and the easier it becomes for them to provide such services. Thus, the constituent game has a snowball effect. It is this effect which, in large part, gives incumbent legislators an advantage over their opponents in winning the next election. Winning that next election is what most state legislators want.

The State Journal-Register

Epilogue: Local Government

Local governments also have legislators. These legislators are the elected members of the county boards, city councils, village boards, school boards, township boards, and special district boards. Like the state legislators, these local legislators make the laws for their local communities and work to provide constituent services for local residents. The work of these local legislators is described in Chapter 7.

The Auditor General

This office is one of the most important in state government, but it is not elective. The auditor general is an officer of the legislative branch and is appointed by the General Assembly for a ten-year term of office.

The auditor general's job is to review the spending of all state funds to see that all money is spent in accordance with the law. The auditor general also reviews the performance of the executive branch — or how agencies carry out the laws of the state to be sure that neither more nor less is done than the laws provide. The auditor general is like a watchdog for the General Assembly, checking especially that the executive branch is doing its job and spending state funds according to the laws and Constitution.

The auditor general is a third financial officer but of the legislative branch, not the executive. The other two state financial officers are elected executive officers: the state treasurer and state comptroller.

How a Bill Becomes Law in Illinois

Source: Legislative Research Unit / Illinois General Assembly

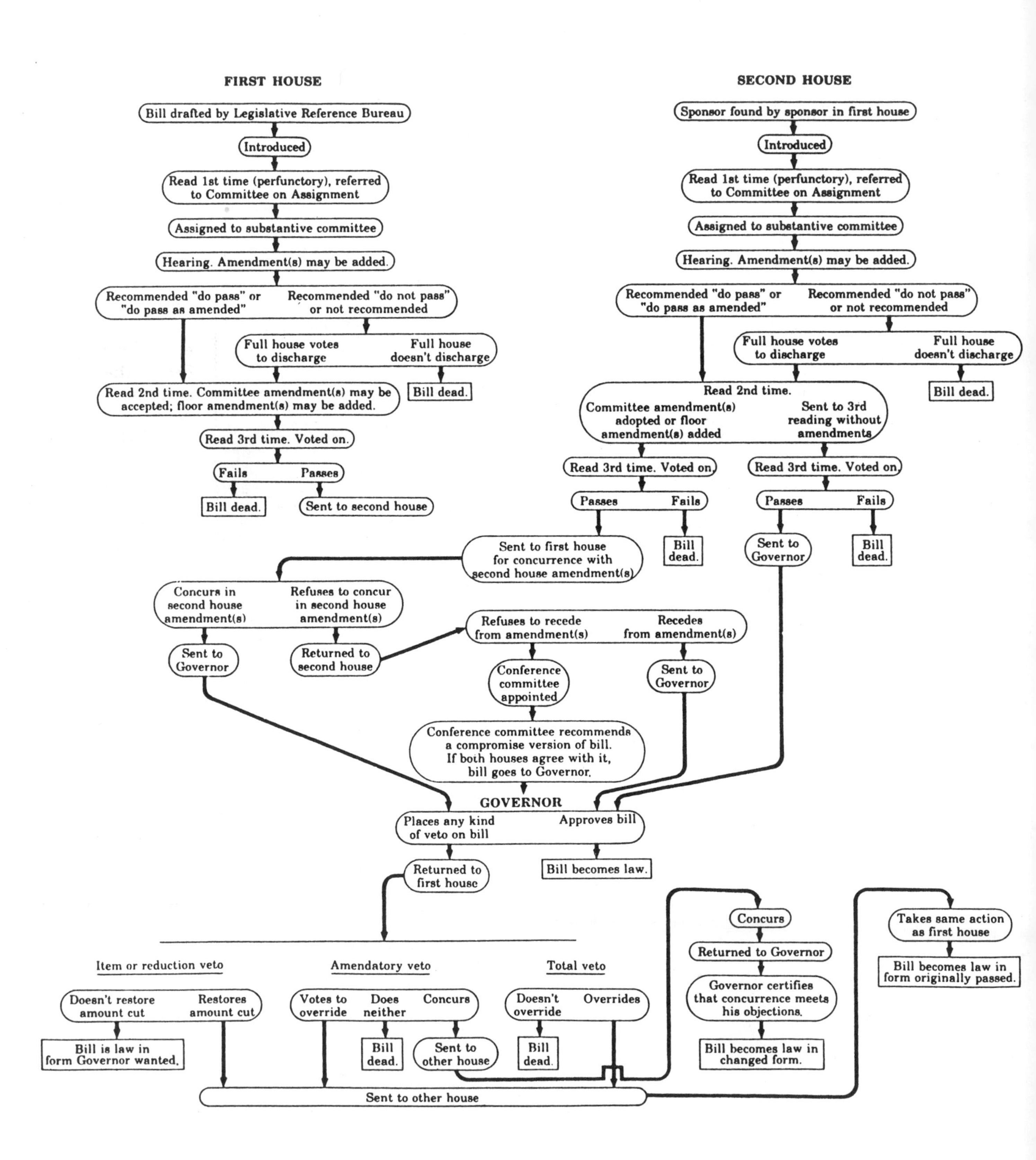

CHAPTER 5

The Governor and the Executive Branch

By Judy Lee (Lewis) Uphoff

From reading the last chapter, you know that the main function of the legislative branch is to pass new laws. Executing those laws is the main function of the executive branch. The word "executing" in the government process means "carrying out" or seeing that laws are put into effect. Laws would only be words on a piece of paper if the executive branch did not see that they went into effect.

Here's another way to understand "executing": If you and your classmates decided to have a party, the party won't happen unless someone takes charge to see that all the arrangements are made. And you would probably want that someone to make sure the party didn't cost more than you had planned to spend.

Electing Illinois' Six Executives

In Illinois, voters elect six state government executive officials: the governor, the lieutenant governor, the secretary of state, the attorney general, the treasurer, and the comptroller. Each is elected at the same time, and each serves a four-year term. (See box, "Illinois' Elected State Executive Officers.") For our national government, there are only two elected executive officials, the president and the vice president.

Illinois' Elected State Executive Officers

Governor	Lieutenant Governor
Attorney General	Secretary of State
Treasurer	Comptroller

Every four years, on the second Monday in January, these six executive officials begin their terms after election the previous November. That November general election is in even-numbered years, in between the elections for U.S. president. That means that Illinois voters elect their state executive officers two years after they voted for the president. Will you be old enough to vote for Illinois' governor and other executive officers by 1994 or the next time in 1998?

To be eligible for each of the executive offices of Illinois, you must be a U.S. citizen, at least 25 years old, and a resident of the state for the three years before the election.

Gov. Jim Edgar, a Republican from Charleston, is the first downstate Illinois governor elected since Louis L. Emmerson of Mount Vernon sixty-two years earlier.

Election of the six executive officials is a two-step process, and in Illinois the elections are very political. First there are primary elections held by the Republican and Democratic parties to nominate their candidates for each office. Then there is the general election when all voters choose between the Republican and Democratic candidates. Each of these executive officials is elected independently of the others, except that the governor and the lieutenant governor candidates of each party must run as a team in the general election. There is no such team requirement in the primaries. (See box, "Primary and General Elections.")

A team requirement prevents election of the governor from one party and the lieutenant governor from another. Because no other candidate for executive office is teamed to the governor, it is not only possible, but probable, that the state's other elected executive officers will be from different parties. For example, in 1982, 1986, and 1990, the Republican candidates won election to the offices of governor, lieutenant governor, and secretary of state, while the Democratic candidates won election to the offices of attorney general, treasurer, and comptroller.

Governor's Office

Standing at the podium of the Illinois House of Representatives, Gov. Jim Edgar presented his first State of the State message to a joint session of the General Assembly on February 13, 1991. Edgar set three main goals for his new administration: limit property tax increases, raise income taxes permanently, and force the state to live within its means.

The Office of Governor

Of all the officials in the Illinois executive branch, the governor is the most prestigious and most powerful. The governor is the chief executive officer of the state of Illinois. Shadrach Bond was the first governor, chosen in 1818 when Illinois became a state. Because citizens in our state still feared rule by kings, early state constitutions would not allow the governor to run for two terms in a row. So, by 1990 Illinois has had thirty-seven governors. The current state Constitution allows governors to run for as many terms as they wish. The governor who has been elected the most times is James R. Thompson, who first took office in January 1977 after the 1976 election. He was reelected three times, with his fourth term ending in January 1991. The newest governor, the thirty-eighth, is Jim Edgar, who was elected in November 1990.

But let's get back to the idea of executing the law. Once a bill becomes law, the governor must see that it is carried out. That is the governor's primary job. Of course, it would be impossible for one person to carry out all the laws of the state. The governor has about 63,500 employees to help, working throughout various executive agencies, departments, commissions, and authorities. The other elected executive officials and their employees also help carry out some of the laws. Each one of these different executive offices has a specific job to do and certain laws to enforce.

Governor's Role in Lawmaking

Besides carrying out the laws, the governor also plays a big role in making the laws. The governor is not a member of the General Assembly, but the governor's executive powers and standing as a political leader give the governor much influence over which bills become laws.

Every year in January the governor makes a speech to the General Assembly called the "State of the State." In this speech the governor suggests to the legislators what legislation to pass. The governor also persuades legislators to introduce bills. The governor has staff assistants who lobby the members of the General Assembly, trying to convince them to approve the bills favored by the governor. When a bill is approved by the General Assembly, it goes to the governor who may sign it into law or veto it.

Governor's Powers To Veto

The power to veto bills passed by the General Assembly is a very important governor's power. By using this power, or threatening to use it, the governor can often pressure the General Assembly to approve legislation in the form that the governor prefers.

The governor of Illinois has more kinds of veto powers than the president of the United States does. Both have the power to veto an entire bill, sending it back to the legislature. The Illinois governor has two other ways to veto bills that authorize spending (called appropriation bills) and another veto power that allows rewriting of bills by the governor.

The State Journal-Register

The first power is the line-item veto. With this power the governor may veto one or more lines of spending amounts for specific programs or projects in one bill, yet the governor can sign the rest of the bill into law. The lines crossed out by the governor are considered vetoed, and that money cannot be spent unless the General Assembly re-passes them with a three-fifths vote in both the Senate and House.

The second power is the reduction veto. With this power, the governor may reduce the amount of money to be spent for a specific program or project. Such a reduction cannot be restored to the amount approved by the General Assembly unless both the House and the Senate re-approve the original amount by a majority vote.

The other veto power allows the governor to write changes into the bills that passed the General Assembly. This power is called the amendatory veto. It allows the governor to write proposed amendments, but only to bills already approved by the General Assembly. This power adds a new dimension to the legislative game in Chapter 5. What if the governor decided not to sign your bill allowing fourteen-year-olds to get driver's licenses? Let's say the governor decided to use the amendatory veto, returning your bill to the General Assembly with a suggested amendment to allow only fourteen-year-olds who are not failing any school work to get a driver's license.

Three things could happen when a bill is returned to the General Assembly with an amendatory veto:

1. The General Assembly could re-pass the original bill, but a three-fifths vote of both houses is required for the original bill to become law.

2. The General Assembly could approve the governor's changes to the bill. A majority vote, not the three-fifths, is needed in both houses for the bill as the governor amended it to become law.

3. The General Assembly could fail to vote either way, and the bill dies.

If the governor neither signs nor vetoes a bill, that bill will become law automatically sixty days after the bill was sent to the governor. The opposite is true if the president neither signs nor vetoes a bill passed by Congress: The bill is vetoed.

Some people believe that the veto powers, particularly the amendatory veto, give the Illinois governor too much power and influence over lawmaking. Others believe that these veto powers are necessary because the General Assembly passes so many bills in the last days of June that it does make mistakes, and the governor can correct any mistakes with vetoes. More important to some is that these veto powers allow the governor to be a strong executive leader, providing a focus for state government decision making.

Primary and General Elections

Each candidate for a state government office in Illinois — in both the legislative and executive branches — must win two elections. First, they must win their party's nomination for the office in their party's primary election. In Illinois, primary elections are held in March followed in November by the general election.

In the primary, each party picks its candidates for office. Usually the Democratic Party and the Republican Party are the major political parties holding primaries. Other parties — generically called "third parties" — can also nominate candidates to run in the general election.

Let's consider the typical Illinois primaries. For instance, if there are three Democrats who want to run for governor, they will run against each other in the Democratic primary election in March. On the same day at the same polling places throughout the state, Republicans who want to be governor will run against each other in the Republican party primary election. In Illinois, voters must declare at the polling place which primary ballot they want — Republican or Democrat. The Democrat who wins the most votes for governor in the Democratic primary wins the party nomination for governor and begins the campaign for the November general election against the Republican who won the Republican Party nomination in the Republican primary.

Sometimes there is no competition at the party primaries for one or more of the state offices. But there always is competition in the general election. Sometimes, too, there are candidates in the general election who are running as members of third parties. These third-party candidates have little chance of winning statewide elections, but if the election is close for one of the offices between the candidates of Republican and Democratic parties, then a third-party candidate could draw just enough votes to have a major influence on which candidate wins the election — and becomes our new state official.

In all Illinois elections, the candidate who gets the most votes is the winner.

Dick Paulus

Governor's Budget Powers

The governor also has important powers over the way the state spends its money. With these powers, the governor can influence and control the kinds of services which the residents of Illinois receive from the state. Only the General Assembly can authorize spending by its approval of appropriation bills, but the governor's line-item and reduction veto powers can make it harder for the General Assembly to re-approve the spending: It takes more votes to override a veto.

Each year, it is the governor who kicks off the process of deciding how much the state will spend on each and every program of the state government. In March each year, the governor presents a spending plan for the state along with a plan for financing it. The plan is called the "state budget," and the governor must balance spending against revenue. A balanced budget means the state will spend no more money in that year than the state expects to receive that year in revenues from taxes, license fees, and other revenue sources.

Bud Roberts / Illinois Army National Guard

The Department of Conservation hosts a Young Hunters Safety Clinic at Camp Lincoln in Springfield, the home of the Illinois Army National Guard. Participants have to pass the course in order to get a hunting license.

To prepare the budget, first the governor must figure out how much money the state of Illinois will receive. That's the total revenue or income. Then the governor divides up that amount for spending by all the state offices and agencies. Because the state is responsible for providing so many things to its citizens, the list for spending is extremely long.

There is education in schools like yours, and in all the state colleges and universities. There are roads and bridges to build or repair. There are some people who need welfare programs for food, housing, clothes, and hospital bills. There are prisons and mental health programs. Business people want help to expand or train workers. Workers want good benefits if they are hurt on the job or help if they lose their jobs. Children need help if someone abuses them. State police are needed to patrol highways. Local governments want financial help from the state, too.

Each agency in Illinois that is funded by the state of Illinois must convince the governor to budget the money it thinks it needs to provide its services. Unless the governor asks for more taxes to increase the revenue side of the budget, there usually is not enough money to spend to satisfy everyone.

The governor sends his budget to the General Assembly, and the General Assembly must authorize all spending by passing appropriations bills. If taxes were proposed, only the General Assembly can approve them. The members of the General Assembly often disagree with the governor's plan for state spending; they also sometimes disagree with the governor's revenue predictions. Finally, the General Assembly passes appropriation bills authorizing spending for the year. If the governor does not like the spending authorized by the General Assembly, the governor can veto appropriation bills (but he cannot increase them).

The governor still has one other important power over spending: the allocation of funds. This means that the governor can still cut back state spending authorized by the General Assembly if the state's income is less than predicted. In short, the governor orders agencies not to spend money.

The Governor's Other Powers

The governor holds much power over state government. The governor appoints the people who run the executive administration agencies, boards, commissions, and authorities — subject to approval by the Senate. If the governor wants to rearrange the powers of the executive agencies, the governor has the power to reorganize them — subject only to the disapproval by either the Senate or the House. The governor can direct

Governor's Office

In his first six weeks in office, Gov. Jim Edgar issued six executive orders. The first, signed January 25, 1991, ordered all offices under his control to continue benefits to military personnel called to duty in the Persian Gulf. That first order also extended the filing date for state income tax returns for all state employees serving in the Gulf. The second executive order issued February 1 dealt with a clarification of the Personnel Rules so that an employee could not resign and then be immediately reinstated in order to cash in unused vacation and sick time. Executive Order Number Three revoked an executive order of former Gov. James R. Thompson that implemented a hiring freeze for all executive positions. On February 15 Gov. Edgar issued a sweeping executive order to reduce by half, by the year 2000, the amount of waste generated by state agencies. The governor also ordered recycling efforts expanded at state offices to include aluminum, corrugated containers, and newspapers. Executive Order Number Five abolished the Governor's Office of Senior Involvement and transferred those duties to the Department on Aging. Similarly, Order Six delegated the powers and duties relating to the Governor's Office of Voluntary Action to the Office of the Lieutenant Governor's Senior Action Centers, thereby abolishing the Governor's Office of Voluntary Action.

the work of state government by issuing executive orders. The governor may also grant pardons to people who have been convicted of crimes in Illinois. And the governor serves as commander-in-chief of the state militia (the National Guard), which can be called out by the governor's order to help if there is a disaster or emergency (or by the president if there is a national emergency and they are needed to help the U.S. Army).

Other Executive Officers

Each of the other five elected executive officials has special duties. We will study these five in the order that they would take over the governorship if something happened to the governor.

The Lieutenant Governor

The lieutenant governor is assigned duties by the governor. Some governors expect the lieutenant governor to do lots of work and others expect very little. The lieutenant governor's job can best be described as an assistant to the governor. The lieutenant governor takes over for the governor when the governor is unable to fulfill the duties, just as the vice president takes over for the president of the United States. Unlike the vice president, who presides over the U.S. Senate and has the power to vote in the Senate to break a tie vote, Illinois' lieutenant governor has no such role.

Lieutenant Governor
Bob Kustra
Republican

The Attorney General

The attorney general is the chief legal officer for the state of Illinois. If Illinois is sued, the attorney general is the state's lawyer. If Illinois as a state must sue because someone did not fulfill a state contract or agreement, the attorney general is the state's lawyer. The attorney general also issues legal opinions for government officials who question new laws or conflicts between state laws. The attorney general keeps records of consumer fraud and helps citizens if they think they have been cheated by a business.

Attorney General
Roland W. Burris
Democrat

The Secretary of State

The secretary of state keeps official records for the state of Illinois. Those records include all the proceedings and decisions of the General Assembly, and all the records on motor vehicle licenses and driver's licenses in Illinois. The offices where you go to take your driver's license test or to get a new driver's license are run by the secretary of state.

The secretary of state is the state archivist and the state librarian. The official state library is administered by the secretary of state, and its literacy programs are available throughout Illinois.

The secretary of state also keeps the records of all rules and regulations that are made by executive branch agencies in carrying out the laws. These are called

Secretary of State George H. Ryan Republican

Comptroller Dawn Clark Netsch Democrat

Treasurer Patrick Quinn Democrat

administrative rules.

The State Comptroller

The state comptroller is one of two state elected financial officers. The comptroller's job is to tell the other financial officer — the state treasurer — what checks to write and which state funds to use in the treasury. The comptroller keeps track of all money spent each year by state government.

The State Treasurer

In Illinois the executive official who actually writes the check is the treasurer. The treasurer also is responsible for the safekeeping and investment of state money.

How They Work Together

Consider how your bill that was passed into law in Chapter 5 would involve these executive officials. What would it take to carry out the law for fourteen-year-olds to get licenses to drive? The governor would have to provide funds in the budget to hire new driver's license examiners to test fourteen-year-olds. The secretary of state would have to hire persons to fill these jobs, train them, and assign them to driver's license examining stations. The comptroller would check to be sure that these persons were officially on the job and review the vouchers from the secretary of state's office for paying their salaries. The comptroller would then tell the treasurer to issue a state check to pay them their salaries. The treasurer would write the checks (or would oversee the electronic writing of these checks) for these examiners. Meanwhile, the attorney general might be defending the new law in court because a fourteen-year-old Illinois driver sideswiped a firetruck in Missouri, where you have to be sixteen to drive a car.

Even though the state executive officials might be from different political parties, once they are elected they must work together to perform their different duties to see that all state laws are "faithfully enforced."

The Administrative Departments

So far we have discussed only the top state elected officials. All of the six elected executive officials have offices in Springfield and Chicago with many people working for them. The governor, as noted at the beginning of this chapter, has by far the most help. These are the 60,000 state employees who work in over 70 executive departments, agencies, boards, commissions, and authorities under the governor. Each of these offices is responsible to the governor. Some are large and some are small. For example, the Department of Corrections, which administers state prisons, has 11,500 employees;

Terry Farmer/Showcase Photography

The new State Library is located just east of the Capitol Complex. Carved into the stone around the top of the library are the names of Illinois' most famous authors.

Illinois Department of Transportation

The Valley City Bridge, here still under construction, is now open and carries traffic on the Central Illinois Expressway, Route 36, over the Illinois River.

the Illinois Racing Board, which regulates horse racing in Illinois, has only one full-time employee.

The Code Departments

Most of the state's services and programs are provided by the state's twenty-six "code" departments. They are called code departments because each is created and its powers and duties are established by one set of state laws, called the administrative code. This code also includes some laws applying to all the departments. For example, it sets up the Personnel Code or civil service system under which most of the employees of these departments and others under the governor are supposed to be hired, retained, promoted, and dismissed.

The code departments are the agencies through which the state provides most of its services to its citizens. The code departments include, for example, the Department of Transportation, which builds and maintains state highways; the Department of Public Aid, which administers welfare programs; the Department of Conservation, which manages the state's parks and issues boat licenses; and the Department of Agriculture, which provides assistance to farmers and operates the State Fairs in Springfield and Du Quoin. All code departments are listed in the box, "Illinois' Code Departments." Can you guess what each of these departments does? Your teacher may have a copy of the *Handbook of Illinois Government* which describes each agency. Every detail about executive agencies is spelled out in the statutes of Illinois government.

Each of these department directors is appointed by the governor with approval of the Senate. The directors are similar to the president's cabinet of the U.S. government.

Dick Paulus

Illinois Department of Conservation

This woman is fishing in one of Illinois' many state parks. The Department of Conservation manages over 260 sites, which encompass 400,000 land acres and 81,000 water acres.

Illinois Department of Public Aid

These 1990 graduates of Joliet West High School took part in Project Pride, a volunteer program of the Illinois Department of Public Aid. Each graduate is given a satin jacket.

Illinois Department on Aging

Community-based services such as meals, transportation, information and referral, legal assistance, and other services that help older people remain independent are provided by the Department on Aging.

Executive Boards

Not all the other Illinois executive or administrative departments are set up with one top person who has the power to make the major decisions. Illinois has many boards and commissions, whose members are appointed by the governor — with consent of the Senate. The members of the board make the major decisions, and usually the board appoints a person as the director in charge of all the employees that work for the board.

Some of these boards are for education. One of the most important is the State Board of Education which coordinates all public education from pre-school through grade twelve. The board appoints the state superintendent of education, who administers all the programs and the employees of the State Board of Education.

There is a separate Illinois Board of Higher Education which oversees the state's higher education system. That system includes the Illinois Student Assistance Commission, which grants financial aid; the Illinois Community College Board, which assists all the local community colleges in the state; and four different university governing boards which run the state's twelve universities. One exception to the governor's appointment of board members is the University of Illinois Board of Trustees whose members are elected statewide by Illinois voters. Still, each of the university boards seeks approval by the governor of its budget and new programs through the Illinois Board of Higher Education.

Illinois Department of Alcoholism and Substance Abuse

Young people march in Grant Park, Chicago, to support "Just Say No" Day. This is an example of many activities organized by the Department of Alcoholism and Substance Abuse to promote healthy lifestyles and alternatives to alcohol and drug abuse.

Illinois' Code Departments

Department on Aging
Department of Agriculture
Department of Alcoholism & Substance Abuse
Department of Central Management Services
Department of Children and Family Services
Department of Commerce and Community Affairs
Department of Conservation
Department of Corrections
Department of Employment Security
Department of Energy & Natural Resources
Department of Financial Institutions
Department of Human Rights
Department of Insurance
Department of Labor
Department of the Lottery
Department of Mental Health
and Developmental Disabilities
Department of Mines and Minerals
Department of Nuclear Safety
Department of Professional Regulation
Department of Public Aid
Department of Public Health
Department of Rehabilitation Services
Department of Revenue
Department of State Police
Department of Transportation
Department of Veterans' Affairs

Governor's Bureau of the Budget

A most important state agency that works directly for the governor is the Bureau of the Budget. This agency is part of the governor's office staff. It works directly for the governor, who gets to hire the director and staff with no approval by the Senate or anyone else. This bureau helps the governor to prepare the state budget. Every other agency sends its budget requests to the Bureau of the Budget. This agency helps the governor to both regulate state spending and to carefully check if revenues will be enough for the state to do all its business throughout the year. The director of the Bureau of the Budget is one of the most important advisers working directly for the governor.

Other Agencies, Boards, and Commissions

The importance of all the departments, agencies, boards, commissions, and authorities to any one citizen may depend on his or her interests. In carrying out the laws, these departments, agencies, etc., also may make administrative rules. The rules help provide detailed guidelines for the laws passed by the legislature.

Another important board appointed by the governor is the State Board of Elections, which administers all of the election laws of the state. It has the official results of all the state elections.

The Illinois National Guard is run by the Military Department, which is headed by the state's adjutant general. The National Guard, as the state's militia, can be called out by the governor to help in case of severe floods or other emergencies. It can also be subject to order by the president, as commander-in-chief of the U.S. military, to be called out to join the nation's regular armed forces.

The state has two important agencies in the environmental field. One is the Illinois Environmental Protection Agency and the other is the Pollution Control Board.

There are boards that regulate certain activities for the state: horse racing, liquor sales, and utility rates on electricity, telephone calls, etc. A commissioner regulates state banks, and another commissioner regulates state savings and loans. There is a council to check on costs of health care.

There are nine authorities, which are like boards, to handle special financing for such things as toll roads, farm loans, business loans, and housing.

There are agencies involved in public safety such as the state fire marshal and the Emergency Services and Disaster Agency.

Interested in the arts or historic preservation? There is an Illinois Arts Council and a Historic Preservation Agency.

The operation of such a vast administrative organization in the Illinois executive branch is a big enterprise. Indeed, the state spends over $26 billion a year operating state government and providing services to Illinois residents through these many agencies. Many state services are provided indirectly through local governments, just as some of the money spent by the Illinois state government comes from the U.S. government.

Bill Campbell

The State Journal-Register

Terry Farmer / Showcase Photography

Ships from all over the world, as well as from other ports on the Great Lakes, dock at Iroquois Landing Lakefront Terminus near Calumet Harbor in Chicago. This terminus is owned by the Illinois International Port District, which is regulated by a nine-member board (four are appointed by the governor and five by the mayor of Chicago), and operated by a stevedoring company.

David C. Tonge

Drivers must pay a fee before they are allowed to use a toll highway. This shows traffic stopping at the Des Plaines toll booths on the Northwest Tollway, I-90, in late winter 1989. According to the Illinois State Toll Highway Authority, the government body responsible for administering the system of four toll highways in the collar counties around Chicago, the revenue for 1989 was $212 million. Part of the money collected goes to pay off the debt incurred in building the roads, and the rest goes to pay for maintenance and operating costs. The newest toll road in the 273.4 mile system is the North-South Tollway, Interstate 355.

Illinois Historic Preservation Agency

Lincoln's New Salem State Historic Site in Petersburg is administered by the Illinois Historic Preservation Agency.

Illinois Historic Preservation Agency

Jordbruksdagama, meaning sorghum pressing in Swedish, is one of the activities recreated at Bishop Hill, a settlement established by Swedish religious dissidents in 1846. Many of the original colony's buildings, including the Old Colony Church and the Bjorklund Hotel, are still functioning, and many of Bishop Hill's 131 residents are descendants of the original settlers. The Bishop Hill State Historic Site is administered by the Illinois Historic Preservation Agency. One attraction of the site is the new museum displaying more than ninety folk art paintings by Olof Krans, an original settler who painted the people and village of Bishop Hill in the 1860s.

CHAPTER 6

The Courts and the Concept of Law

By Denny L. Schillings

Law is an important and common part of our everyday lives, but we seldom give much thought to it. In very general terms, law is a rule that allows human beings to live together in some kind of orderly manner. Laws have been around as long as mankind. Some of the earliest references to written laws come from ancient history. King Hammurabi of ancient Babylon formally established a code of law as early as 2250 B.C. The Greeks philosophized about the effect of good and bad laws. Roman law was a keystone in the rule of the empire for over 1,000 years. Written, organized, and generally accepted laws written by legislatures, like the ones we are accustomed to, are relatively new to world history, however.

While using many of the ideas of the Greeks, Romans, and others, the framers of our U.S. Constitution looked most often to England. By the year 1150 A.D., the English were living under a government with a single ruler, and laws were applied throughout the nation. A variety of laws, called the Common Law, had been developing for centuries and were established for all to follow as judges made decisions in England.

You have learned that our laws are passed by the representatives of the people — the Congress and the state legislatures or county boards and municipal councils. But it is the courts which both interpret the laws and decide the guilt or innocence of people charged with breaking the laws.

The basic concept of federalism, which we studied in Chapter 3, is easily identified in our court system. Our national court system deals with federal law and interprets the U.S. Constitution. The state courts interpret state and local laws and the state Constitution. Some cases from state courts can also be appealed through the federal system. Anytime a state or local law is challenged as being in violation of the U.S. Constitution, the case may go through the federal judiciary. But, for the most part, the state and local laws that govern our everyday lives are left up to the state courts.

Civil and Criminal Law

Laws are divided into two broad types. State courts deal with both. The first, civil law, involves disputes between two or more individuals or groups. If you were involved in an automobile accident and sued the other person for damages, it would be a civil law case. Another example could involve a contract. Assume your mother signed a contract to have a new roof put on your house, and the roofer did not complete the work. Your mother might bring a civil suit against the roofer to get her money back or force the roofer to finish the job. In both examples the civil law involved deals with relationships between individuals, NOT CRIMES.

Dick Paulus

Criminal law is the other type. When citizens actually break a law, the state brings charges against them. A "misdemeanor" is a crime that is not too serious, and it does not involve a large fine or long jail term. Shoplifting is an example. If found guilty, the person might be sentenced to probation or fined. The punishment is meant to discourage the person from criminal actions in the future.

A "felony," on the other hand, is a serious criminal act such as robbery, murder, or arson. Felonies have much more severe penalties than misdemeanors. Long prison terms and large fines are common for those convicted of a felony. A person who has committed a felony is said to have harmed society as a whole, and the punishment is meant to protect society from further injury.

The Judicial System in Illinois

Article VI of the Illinois Constitution establishes a system of courts for the state. In many ways the state court system is similar in purpose and structure to that of the federal system. Both have three basic levels; both interpret the constitution for their respective jurisdictions; and both are responsible for deciding individual cases that come before them. The federal and state judiciaries are the third branch of government created by the separation of powers doctrine, providing checks and balances to the powers of the executive and legislative branches of the government.

There are also differences between the state and federal court systems just as there are with the two other branches. The responsibilities of the federal court system are broadly defined because its decisions affect all the states, as well as other countries, as it interprets and applies federal laws and the U.S. Constitution. The responsibility of the Illinois court system, on the other hand, is rather detailed because it deals with state laws that concern nearly all aspects of our lives. Another difference between the state and federal judiciary is the number and type of courts. The U.S. Congress is given power to create lower courts if it thinks they are needed. In Illinois, the entire court system is set out in the state Constitution; the General Assembly cannot create any other courts. A final difference is that judges in Illinois are elected for a specific term of office, whereas federal judges are appointed for life. Illinois' system of elected judges is discussed later in this chapter.

The federal judicial system was set up in Article III of the U.S. Constitution. There is a nine-member Supreme Court empowered to make final judgment on cases appealed to it. Any other federal courts were left up to Congress to establish, and it did so in 1789 by passing the Judiciary Act.

The act created a system of lower federal courts to assist the Supreme Court in dealing with federal laws. In each state there is at least one U.S. District Court, and most federal cases start at this level. For Illinois there are three U.S. District Courts. The Northern District has offices in Chicago and Rockford; the Central District has offices in Peoria, Springfield, Rock Island, and Danville; and the Southern District has offices in East St. Louis, Benton, and Alton. If the decision of the District Court is challenged, the case goes up to the next level — to one of thirteen U.S. Courts of Appeals. If the decision of the Appeals Court is challenged, the case goes up to the U.S. Supreme Court. In addition, Congress has created a number of specialized courts such as military courts, the U.S. Court of International Trade,

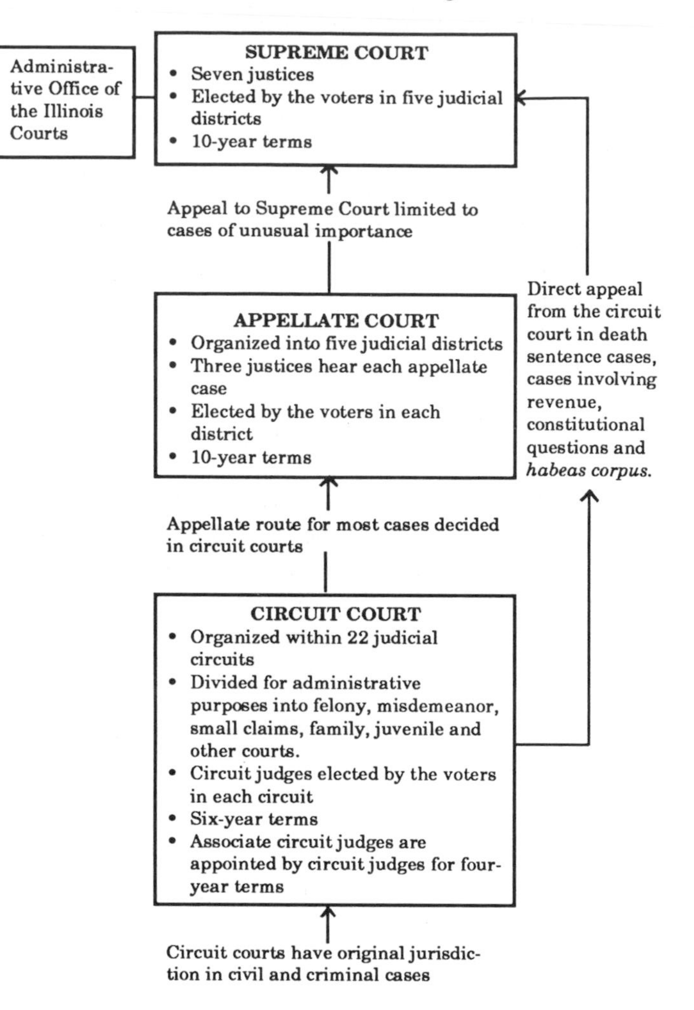

U.S. Tax Court, and the U.S. Territorial District Courts. It is the U.S. Supreme Court that makes the final decisions on any challenges made to decisions of these courts.

Circuit Courts

The lowest level of Illinois' three-tiered court system is the Circuit Court, sometimes called trial courts. Circuit Courts hear cases of all kinds, from divorces to murders. The Circuit Courts have original jurisdiction in both civil and criminal cases.That means the Circuit Courts are the first courts where both civil and criminal cases are tried. They are the most numerous of all the state courts. The state is divided into twenty-two areas called judicial circuits, and each contains one or more counties. The largest of these circuits, in population but not land, is Cook County (where Chicago is located). Du Page County, the second most populous county, also has its own circuit, as does Will County. The other nineteen circuits contain two or more counties.

The Constitution further states that there will be at least one circuit court judge for every county. For Cook County thirty-six circuit judges must come from Chicago and twelve from the rest of the county. It is left up to the General Assembly to provide for more circuit court judges, and it has. In 1990, there were nearly 400 circuit court judges holding court in the twenty-two circuits. Circuit court judges are elected by the voters in their circuit for six-year terms. They are nominated in their political party primary election and, to become judge, must win the general election. If they want to serve another term, their names go directly on the general election ballot and no one can run against them. Instead, voters mark the ballot either yes or no to retain the judge for another term. Three-fifths or more of the voters actually participating in the election must vote in favor of retaining the judge for the judge to get another term.

The Illinois Constitution also provides for another type of circuit court judge, called associate judges. They are appointed by the elected circuit court judges for a term of four years. Some people criticize how the appointments are made since there are no guarantees the person appointed will make a good judge. Of course, circuit court judges are elected through the political process, and this leads to other criticism that these judges could be too political.

The associate judge's role in the Circuit Court system is to hear cases concerning traffic tickets, charges of disorderly conduct, drunken driving, and other offenses that carry less severe penalties than other more serious offenses. The legislature has authorized the appointment of nearly 350 associate judges. Because of their role in dealing with minor offenses, associate judges are the most familiar to many Illinois residents.

In order for the Circuit Court system to better serve the public, each circuit is divided into divisions. One division may hear felony cases, another only juvenile cases, yet another only divorces. As cases come to the Circuit Court, the chief judge of the circuit assigns each to a specific court and judge. A chief judge is elected for each circuit by the circuit judges in that circuit. The chief judge is extremely important because he or she is in charge of seeing that all the cases move smoothly through the system.

Photos by Terry Farmer/Showcase Photography

The Illinois Supreme Court does not allow photographs to be taken of circuit court trials, but Sangamon County Circuit Court Judge Richard J. Cadagin arranged for these "staged" photos to show his courtroom. At top, Judge Cadagin is at right, talking to an attorney who has approached the bench. Seated at far left is the court reporter, and in the middle is the court clerk with the sheriff's bailiff behind her. The middle photo illustrates what often happens in court. The judge hears from the lawyers for both sides (the defense and the prosecution in a criminal case, the plaintiff and the defendant in a civil case). At bottom is the Sangamon County Courthouse, where the circuit court is located and county officials have their offices.

The Appellate Courts

Most cases are settled at the Circuit Court level, but every citizen has the right to ask for another chance to be heard if the case was decided against him or her. The method to achieve another hearing is called an appeal, and the state court set up to hear appeals is the Appellate Court. It is the second of the three tiers.

Article VI, Sections 5 and 6 of the Illinois Constitution establishes the Appellate Court. The Constitution created five Appellate Court districts. Cook County, because of its large population compared to the rest of the state, was established as one district all by itself. The rest of the counties are divided into the other four districts, which are to be about the same in population.

Each Appellate Court may hold court anywhere within its district boundaries. The First District courtrooms are all in Chicago; the Second District meets in Elgin; the Third District has court in Ottawa; the Fourth District sits in Springfield; and the Fifth District meets in Mount Vernon. Normally, a case heard by the Appellate Court would have been tried in one of the Circuit Courts within its boundaries.

Like circuit court judges, appellate court judges are elected, but for terms of ten years. There are thirty-six elected appellate court judges in Illinois—sixteen in the First District, six in the Second and Fifth districts, and four in the Third and Fourth districts. (Other appellate judges are assigned or appointed by the Illinois Supreme Court.)

In some ways the Appellate Court system is simpler than the Circuit Court system. With five, rather than twenty-two districts, the number of individuals needed to run the court is much smaller. The Appellate Court judges in each district appoint a clerk and other personnel as needed. Similar to the Circuit Court's chief judge, the appellate judges in each district pick a presiding judge to administer cases.

The Circuit Court and Appellate Court handle cases in different ways. At the Circuit Court level, a single judge hears the case, weighs the evidence, checks and interprets the laws that apply, and makes a decision, often aided by the use of a jury. If a case reaches the Appellate Court, only the lawyers are present, and they present the case to a panel of three judges. In order for a decision to be made, two of the three appellate judges must agree.

The Illinois Supreme Court

Article VI of the state Constitution also establishes the Illinois Supreme Court as the highest court in the state. The Constitution gives the Illinois Supreme Court original jurisdiction in a few instances such as cases involving revenue (tax collection or expenditures). Basically, the Supreme Court, which meets both in Springfield and Chicago, is the highest appeals court in the state at the top of the three tiers.

Unlike the Appellate Courts, which must accept all cases of appeal from the Circuit Courts, the Supreme Court has the right to decide which cases of appeal it will hear, with one exception: It must hear any case from the Circuit Court when the death penalty is imposed.

Terry Farmer / Showcase Photography

The Illinois Supreme Court Building in Springfield is at the corner of Capitol Avenue and Second Street, across the street from the Capitol. The Illinois Supreme Court also has offices in downtown Chicago in the Richard J. Daley Center on the thirtieth floor.

There are seven Illinois Supreme Court judges, called justices, and all seven hear and decide every case that comes before the court. Whereas federal Supreme Court justices are appointed for life, Illinois elects its Supreme Court justices for terms of ten years. The five Appellate Court districts are also used for electing Supreme Court justices. Cook County elects three Supreme Court justices, and each of the other four districts elects one.

The three levels of courts are one unified system under the Supreme Court. Every three years the seven justices decide which one of them will be chief justice of the Illinois Supreme Court. The chief justice is responsible not only for administration of the Supreme Court, but also is in charge of the entire Illinois court system. It is the job of the chief justice to prepare a budget for operating the court system and to make sure that each court performs its constitutional duties.

The Power over All Laws

Most of the disputes that come before our state and federal courts deal with decisions based on the application of laws: Either the law was broken or improperly followed, or it was not. A small number of cases, however, involve constitutional issues. When the court decides issues of constitutionality, it is called "judicial review." The power of judicial review is not spelled out in either the U.S. or Illinois constitutions. But in a series of cases in the early nineteenth century, the U.S. Supreme Court established its power to review the constitutionality of laws made by the Congress. If a law is found to be in conflict with the U.S. Constitution, the U.S. Supreme Court may declare the law no longer in force. The Constitution of Illinois operates on this same basic idea, and the ultimate authority for deciding that state or local laws do not conflict with the Illinois Constitution rests with the Illinois Supreme Court. In this way the judiciary is a very powerful tool in assuring that the legislature passes no laws that violate its powers under the Constitution.

Attorney General and State's Attorney

While the Illinois judicial system is established by the state Constitution, the actual function of the system involves many more individuals. The chief lawyer in Illinois is the attorney general. Elected statewide as a part of the executive branch, the attorney general is responsible for representing the state, or its officials, in lawsuits. He also advises the state's attorneys in the 102 Illinois counties.

Section 19 of Article VI requires that a state's attorney be elected in each county. The state's attorney is exactly what the title implies, the attorney for the state in criminal and civil matters within a county. Since the state has its own attorney, anyone accused of a serious crime by the state has the right to be represented by an attorney also. Sometimes an individual cannot afford to hire an attorney, however, and the chief judge of the Circuit Court appoints a public defender. Most counties have regular public defenders. In less populous counties, the court will pay a private attorney to be a public defender.

Other Court Employees

In order to further help the court run smoothly, several other people are important. To make a record of everything that is said in court the chief judge appoints

Herbert Georg Studio / Illinois Supreme Court

The Illinois Supreme Court's official photograph taken in January 1991 (after three new justices took office in December following their election in November 1990) shows the seven justices at the bench in the Supreme Court Building in Springfield. From left are Justice James D. Heiple, Justice Horace L. Calvo, Justice William G. Clark, Chief Justice Benjamin K. Miller, Justice Thomas J. Moran, Justice Michael A. Bilandic, and Justice Charles E. Freeman. The three newly elected justices are Heiple, Bilandic, and Freeman.

a court reporter. Court reporters are present at all sessions of the Circuit Court.

Every four years a circuit clerk is elected to serve in each of the circuits. The circuit clerk is responsible for keeping the records made by the reporters and any evidence submitted in a case. Since the organization of records is important, the circuit clerk appoints deputy clerks to serve in every courtroom in the circuit.

Although elected as a county and not a Circuit Court official, one of the sheriff's responsibilities is to help the Circuit Court. The sheriff and his deputies serve orders and warrants issued by the judges. To keep order and protect the judge, the sheriff appoints deputies to act as court bailiffs. Although appointed by the sheriff, the bailiff is an employee of the court.

Bill Campbell

Choosing Our Judges

Every state has its own set of standards to become a judge. In Illinois, all judges must be licensed attorneys-at-law under Illinois regulations. They must be citizens of Illinois and live in the judicial area from which they are elected or appointed. Once an attorney becomes a judge, he or she may not carry on a private practice and must devote full-time to court duties. In order to further avoid any conflicts of interest, anyone serving as a judge may not be elected to any other office. The judge is our most obvious and public link to the ideals expressed in our constitutions. Because of his or her position in the interpretation of law and the application of justice under those laws, the character and reputation of a judge must be beyond question.

Election v. Appointment of Judges

One of the continuing controversies in Illinois is the method used to select our judges. To become a judge, an attorney must be nominated, campaign, and be elected. In order to remain a judge at the end of a term, the judge must run for retention of the office on the regular election ballot. Critics say that the system makes judgeships far too political since the candidates are nominated in political party primaries, and they run in the general election under a specific political party label. Supporters of the elective system say judges should be chosen by citizens because choosing them any other way could lead to control of the process by elite groups. Supporters say that both political parties reflect widely held attitudes. Critics argue that judges should hold their positions based on knowledge of the law, not on how well they campaign or on whether their party is the dominant one within the circuit or district. Critics contend that few voters know the judicial candidates or their qualifications, which defeats the purpose of the election process. When running for retention, the judge must receive three-fifths "yes" votes. Seldom if ever is the courtroom record of a judge discussed during a campaign, and voters often skip the retention question for a judge on ballots. Only a handful of judges in Illinois have failed to win retention.

Critics of electing judges have proposed that judges be appointed based on a system called merit selection. There are several variations of such systems used in other states. Generally, the governor would be given a list of qualified attorneys after a special commission has searched through their achievements and experience as lawyers. The governor would then appoint the judges, usually to a specified term.

Those in favor of the elective system maintain it is the most democratic and representative method possible. Judges, because they are deciding cases, are in fact making law by interpreting it, and the people should have a voice to influence the law. Through election, they argue, judges are held accountable for their decisions: Good judges are kept, and bad ones rejected.

The only way to change the entire Illinois system of electing judges is by amending the state Constitution. A proposed amendment can be placed on the ballot by the General Assembly for the voters of Illinois to approve or reject. In 1970, when voters ratified the state Constitution, they were offered the separate question of appointing judges. The voters rejected the merit appointment of judges.

The Jury

There are many more parts of the courts and judicial system that we could study. One of the most important is the jury. The right to a trial by jury is guaranteed to citizens. The Sixth Amendment of the U.S. Constitution says that "... the accused shall enjoy the right to a speedy and public trial, by an impartial jury of the State and district wherein the crime shall have been committed ...." The Seventh Amendment guarantees the right to a jury in civil cases. The Illinois Constitution also ensures this right in Article I.

The jury at a trial is formally known as a petit jury, or small jury. In Illinois, the petit jury consists of twelve persons who have certain qualifications. Jurors must be at least eighteen years old and able to understand the English language. In addition, they must be a resident and registered voter in Illinois. Jurors are called for service by a random selection from the list of registered voters.

The petit jury hears and decides both civil and criminal cases. The petit jurors serve for two weeks at a time, but if the trial continues beyond that time the juror is required to remain until it is over. In Illinois, unanimous agreement by the jurors is needed for a conviction.

The other type of jury in Illinois is a grand jury. The grand jury consists of twenty-three persons, chosen in the same way as a petit jury. The grand jury does not sit in a trial like a petit jury. The grand jury hears the state's attorney, also called the prosecutor, present evidence involving a crime. It is the grand jury that decides whether or not there is sufficient evidence to issue an indictment (formal charge of guilt). Once an indictment has been issued, the individual is required to stand trial, and the normal trial sequence begins.

Although the grand jury is mentioned specifically in the U.S. Constitution, it does not require that a state call one. Illinois does not use statewide grand juries; Illinois has grand juries called by counties for serious violations of the law. Since the grand jury meets in secret to hear the prosecutor's evidence without the defendant or his attorney present, it can hear evidence not normally allowed in an open trial. Based on the information brought to it, the grand jury has the power to conduct its own investigation, calling witnesses and gathering evidence. Using information it receives in such a fashion, it can then issue a formal accusation of guilt if necessary. This method has been used effectively when dealing with underworld criminals, drug traffickers, white-collar criminals, or corrupt government officials. The grand jury normally sits for thirty days, but it can sit as long as eighteen months.

The Illinois Court System in Action

We have looked at the various parts of the judicial system in Illinois, but an example of how it works in a criminal case should help you understand it better.

Bill Small was a nineteen-year-old high school dropout. After three years of part-time jobs he was unemployed and broke. In order to get money, he decided to rob a neighborhood gas station. On a Monday night, just after eleven, Bill put on a Halloween mask and set out to gain quick money.

As he walked toward the gas station, Bill was not aware that a city police officer on routine patrol had spotted him. Bill forced the attendant on duty to empty the cash register. Then Bill ran out of the station with the money in his pocket. The police were waiting outside.

"Drop your weapon," the police officer commanded. "I don't have one," answered Bill. The officer arrested him, reading to Bill his rights at the same time: He could remain silent; any answers he gave could be used against him in court; he could be represented by an attorney; and, if he could not afford an attorney, one would be provided free. The officer then asked, "Do you understand these rights?" Bill said, "Yes."

Handcuffed and riding in the back of the squad car, Bill was taken to the police station to be booked. Since this was his first felony arrest, the police did not have identification materials available on him. So, soon after entering the station house, Bill was fingerprinted, photographed, and asked for his address. The rest of the night was spent looking at the inside of the temporary holding cell in the police station.

On Tuesday morning Bill was taken to a courtroom for a bail bond hearing. At the hearing a judge said Bill could be released on bail until time to go to trial if he paid an amount of money. His bail was set at $5,000, but he was told only ten percent, or $500, was needed to post his bail and be free until the trial. Bill told the judge that he had no money for bail or an attorney. Bill was returned to his temporary holding cell, and a public defender came to see him. Bill explained what he had done to his attorney, the public defender, and the public defender explained that Bill would go to court again the next day.

Wednesday, with the courts in full session, Bill was taken, along with his public defender, to a preliminary hearing. The judge heard the state's attorney present the evidence and decided there was reason to believe Bill may be guilty. Bill was then taken into another court room for arraignment where formal charges would be made against Bill. Since this was Bill's first arrest on any felony charge, his attorney explained to Bill that the charges against him would be read. His attorney further advised Bill that he would be required to plead either guilty or not guilty.

Somewhat confused, and very scared, Bill asked what he should do. If he said he was not guilty, a trial would be ordered, he was told. If he were to plead guilty, he could waive his right for a jury trial and be tried before a judge. Given the circumstances, he was advised by his attorney to plead guilty and let his attorney try to get a reduced sentence. Bill decided the advice was probably good, and he agreed to admit to the crime. The arraignment was over. He was scheduled to appear before the circuit court judge a week later.

The following Wednesday, Bill was escorted to the circuit court room. Before he arrived, his lawyer (the public defender) had talked to the prosecutor (the state's attorney). When Bill arrived in court, his attorney explained that he had "plea bargained," or made a deal with the state's attorney. Since Bill was going to plead guilty and it was his first offense, the state's attorney had agreed to ask the judge for a reduced sentence.

Soon, standing before the judge, Bill heard the charges read against him. Once more the judge asked if he were guilty as charged. Bill said "yes." Since Bill had fulfilled his part of the bargain, the state's attorney asked the judge for a reduced sentence. The judge agreed and ordered a three-year probation. Bill's attorney explained that he would have to report, once each week, to a specially appointed officer of the court. This probation officer would help him find a job but would also check on him to make sure that Bill stayed out of trouble. If Bill failed to report regularly to his probation officer, he would most likely go to prison, he was told.

Now with a criminal court record and on probation, Bill could see that his quick money scheme had not been very wise. But at least he was not in prison, and someone would try to help find him a job, and maybe things would begin to improve.

Bill's story is a fairly simple one, but it shows the many checks in our court system. At each turn he was advised of his rights, given the opportunity of a jury trial, and finally given a reasonable punishment for his crime. If the case had gone to trial with Bill pleading innocent, and if he was found guilty, Bill still had the right to appeal the decision.

If Bill had been younger, less than age seventeen, he would have gone through the Illinois juvenile court procedures. They are intended to be protective of children, even those who commit serious crimes. In all cases, whether a trial is conducted before a judge or jury, the purpose is the same — to enforce the laws of society and to protect individual rights before the law. Remember, a key principle behind the federal and state judicial systems is that an individual is innocent until proven guilty. With that in mind, we have a system that does everything possible to protect the accused from wrongful conviction. The courts can be just and fair if the laws are good, and the legislative branch is responsible for making good laws.

Miranda v. Arizona

On March 3, 1963, an eighteen-year-old woman in Phoenix, Arizona, was kidnapped and raped. Two weeks later, police arrested Ernesto Miranda. They took him to the police station, where the victim identified him in a lineup. He was taken into a separate room, and for the next two hours, police questioned him concerning the crime.

At first Miranda denied guilt, but eventually he was convinced to confess. The case seemed to be a closed matter; only conviction in court was left.

At Miranda's trial, the confession was used as evidence against him. He was convicted and sentenced to prison. It appeared that the police and court had done their jobs well. Miranda's attorneys were not convinced, however, that the law had been carried out properly.

Miranda's attorney (also called counsel) pointed out that at no time, either when arrested or during questioning at the police station, had he been advised of his constitutional rights. In addition, he had not been advised that counsel could be present during the interrogation. His rights had been violated, and the confession constituted self-incrimination, which is prohibited by the U.S. Constitution.

The Arizona Supreme Court heard the appeal the following year and upheld the original conviction. Still not convinced that Miranda was given the rights guaranteed him by the Constitution, counsel for Miranda appealed the case further. The U.S. Supreme Court agreed to review the appeal in the spring of 1966.

On June 13, 1966, the U.S. Supreme Court overturned the conviction of Ernesto Miranda, pointing out that while there was no indication that force was used to obtain the confession, Miranda had unknowingly testified against himself by signing the confession. The Supreme Court also agreed that Miranda was not given an opportunity to consult with an attorney at any time before or during the questioning. Without making clear statements to a suspect concerning his rights, any evidence, including a confession, could not be used in a trial. The court then gave police specific procedures to use when arresting a criminal. The result has become known popularly as the "Miranda Warning."

Custodial Interrogation (Miranda) Warning

After each part of the following warning, the officer must determine whether the suspect understands what he or she is being told:

1. You have the right to remain silent. You do not have to talk to me unless you want to do so.
2. If you do want to talk to me, I must advise you that whatever you say can and will be used as evidence against you in court.
3. You have a right to consult with a lawyer and to have a lawyer present with you while you are being questioned.
4. If you want a lawyer but are unable to pay for one, a lawyer will be appointed to represent you free of any cost to you.
5. Knowing these rights, do you want to talk to me without having a lawyer present? You may stop talking to me at any time and you may also demand a lawyer at any time.

Source: Police Training Institute, University of Illinois.

CHAPTER 7

Illinois Local Government: Counties, Cities, Villages, Townships, Schools, Etc.

By Darlene Emmert Fisher

It's a lovely spring day. You grab your skateboard and start out with your friends. After a few moments of skateboarding in a local parking lot, the village police show up.

"You can't use those things here. It's against the village ordinances. Move on or we'll have to arrest you."

"Where can you use skateboards?" you ask.

"I don't know. The village council says no skateboarding on public property."

So what can you do? How can you find a place where you and your friends can skateboard?

Perhaps instead, on that lovely morning you go to your local park for your favorite sport. You look around and discover that so many dogs have been to the park already that there is no pleasant place to put your feet. What can you do about it?

Terry Farmer / Showcase Photography

While local ordinances may regulate skateboarding, owners of private property can also prohibit activities that may endanger people. Springfield, for example, bans all skateboarding in its downtown area and on its sidewalks, but private security patrols White Oaks Mall parking lot.

Both situations are controlled by local government. So finding solutions to your problems needs to begin with understanding local government. Local government is the government which is closest to the people, operating at a neighborhood level to provide immediate services to people where they live. Every city and village is a local government. So is every county, township, and school district. You turn to your local government to handle problems closest to you. Consider some of the basic functions of local government in your community: roads, law enforcement, education, water and sewer services, delivery of welfare services, fire protection, parks, recreation programs, and cemeteries.

Local government is the part of government in which it is easiest for you to participate. You or your friends may be appointed to a committee; support a friend as a candidate for office; take part in efforts to influence the decision of the school board, the city council, or the county board; or even run some day for government office yourself. Because the other citizens involved in local government are your neighbors, it is easier to influence them and see the results of that influence than it is to influence the U.S. Congress or the state legislature.

Types of Local Government

In all, Illinois has over 6,600 units of local government, fifty percent more than any other state. Obviously, this chapter cannot describe each of these governments. It will talk about each different kind of local government. It will also give special attention to the city of Chicago and to Cook County. These are such large and complex governments — they serve one-fourth to one-third of the state's total population — that the state has special regulations which apply only to them.

There are four different kinds of local government

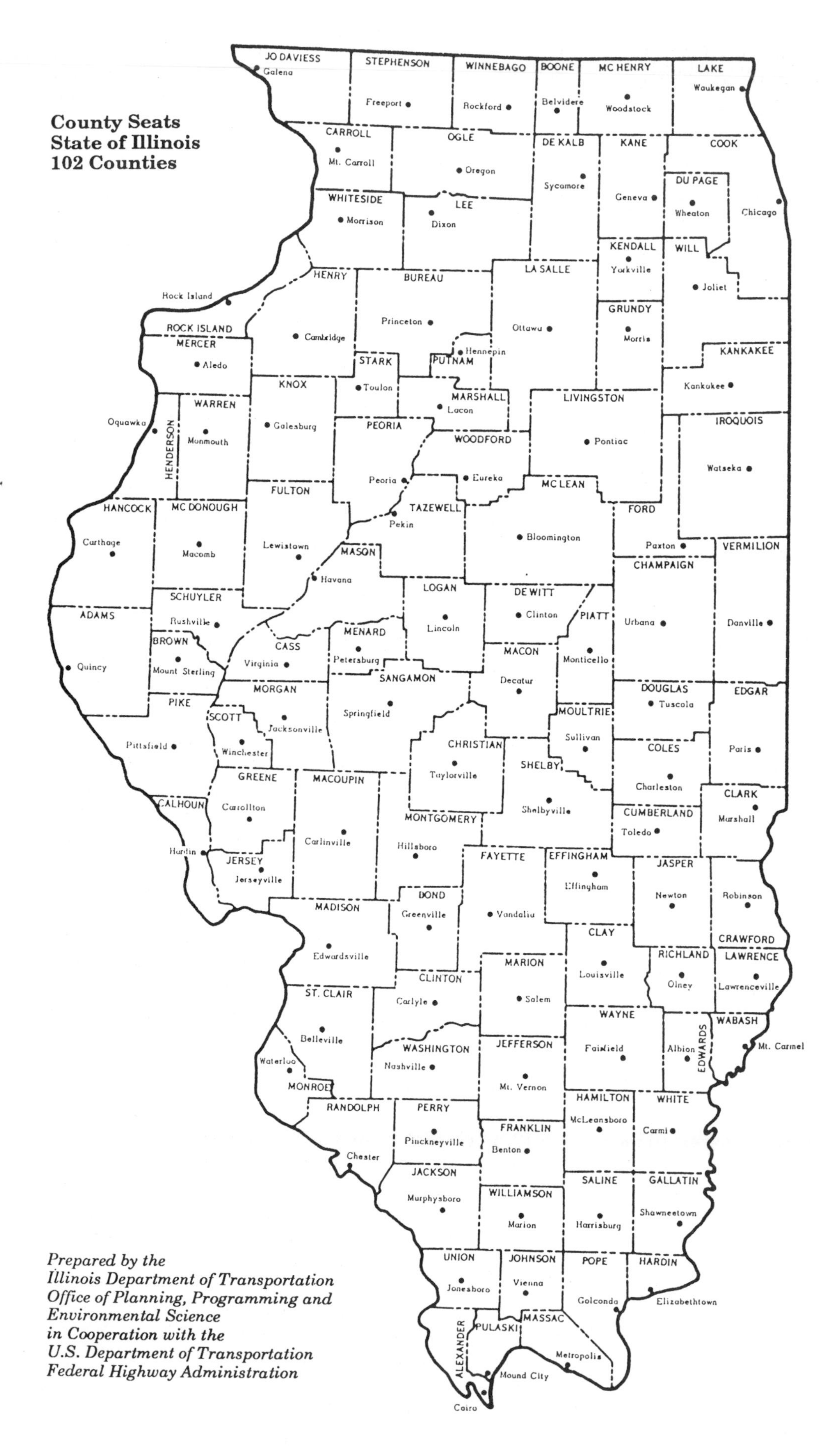

County Seats
State of Illinois
102 Counties

Prepared by the
Illinois Department of Transportation
Office of Planning, Programming and
Environmental Science
in Cooperation with the
U.S. Department of Transportation
Federal Highway Administration

in Illinois: county, municipality, township, and special district.

Counties are the basic unit of local government. All parts of the state are served by a county. Counties administer state services at the local level; they also provide many local services, especially in rural areas.

Cities and villages (both are also called municipalities) are like counties in that they are general purpose governments. They are established to provide the broader range of local services required in urban areas.

Townships are found in eighty-five of Illinois' 102 counties. They provide a limited number of very local services. In Chicago and in the seventeen counties where townships do not exist, those functions are provided by county or municipal governments.

Special districts are found throughout the state. Each special district was established to provide a single service to a particular geographic area. The services which are most often provided through the use of a special district are public education (school districts), parks (park districts), and sewage treatment (sanitary districts).

Counties

Illinois is divided into 102 counties. All parts of the state are located in one of these counties; all municipalities are located in one or more of these counties. (Some municipalities straddle county lines.) Chicago is located in Cook County.

County governments provide such services as law enforcement, roads, health protection, and welfare. Counties are also administrative subdivisions of the state, which means they administer elections; keep birth,

Georgia A. Scobell

The courthouse in Carlinville, county seat for Macoupin County, is famous for its architecture and its cost of construction. E.E. Meyers, who also designed the "new" Capitol in Springfield, was the architect for the state's first million-dollar courthouse in Carlinville. In 1869, Meyers estimated the construction cost at $185,000, but in making the building "fireproof" the cost was over $1.4 million when completed three years later. After forty years of quarrels and scandals, Macoupin County held a two-day celebration in July 1910 when the debt was finally paid off.

death, and other vital records; and house the lowest level of the state's three-part court system, the Circuit Courts.

Each Illinois county has elected administrative officers. Under the Illinois Constitution, each county must elect:

- a sheriff, who is the county's chief law enforcement officer;
- a clerk, who administers elections and keeps the county's records;
- a treasurer, who is custodian of the county's money; and
- a state's attorney, who prosecutes persons accused of crimes and is the county's chief legal officer.

Counties also elect a clerk of the circuit court, who maintains court records, but the General Assembly could change that office to be an appointed one.

Counties have the option of electing a number of other officers, including a recorder to keep track of property records, an auditor to check the accuracy of county financial records, an assessor to calculate the value of taxable real estate, and a coroner to determine the cause of death of persons who die in accidents or under questionable circumstances.

Each county has a legislative body, called the county board, which makes county laws, called ordinances. Each also has an organized method to administer its services. But Illinois counties have different forms of governments, with different relationships between the county board and the administration of services.

Forms of County Government

The most common form of county government in Illinois is the county board. The county board is made up of members elected from districts within the county. (Boards vary in size from fifteen to twenty-nine members.) Board members elect one member to be the county board chair to run their meetings. Each board divides itself into committees, where most of the board's work is performed. Typically, there will be a separate board committee to supervise each of the administrative departments that report to the board.

Two varieties of the county board form have evolved. Instead of a county board chair, in Du Page and St. Clair counties a county board president is elected by the voters of the county. Many county boards are creating the position of county administrative officer, who is hired by the board to help it on important questions, to help prepare and manage the county budget, and to assist in the supervision of administrative departments. Champaign, De Kalb, Madison, McHenry, McLean, Peoria, Rock Island, St. Clair, and Winnebago counties are among the more than twenty counties which currently hire county administrators.

The second basic form of county government is the county commission. In this form, the voters elect a three-member board of commissioners which holds both the legislative and executive powers of the county. Typically, the position of board president is rotated among the commissioners. Each commissioner heads one of the county's administrative departments. The seventeen counties in southern Illinois which do not have township governments use this form of county government.

Illinois law also provides for a county executive form of government. This is like the county board form except that all administrative power is in the hands of a county executive who is elected at-large by the voters of the county. Adoption of this form of government gives a county government home rule powers, but to date no county has adopted it. State law also permits counties to adopt this form while rejecting home rule powers for the county. Will County did this in 1988, and Kane County voters did the same in 1990.

Cook County

Cook County is unique. Cook County has townships in its suburban areas, but it has no township governments within the boundaries of the city of Chicago. The Cook County seventeen-member board is elected from two districts. Chicago forms one district and elects ten members. (In November 1990, voters in Cook County passed a referendum to require that small and equal districts be set up for electing county commissioners.) All of Cook County outside of Chicago forms a second district and elects seven members. The county board serves as a legislative body for the county. The Cook County board president, who is elected by voters in the entire county, is the chief executive officer for the county. Cook County's form of government also guaranteed that it got home rule powers when the 1970 Illinois Constitution was adopted.

Cook County also has eight other elected administrative officials: sheriff, county clerk, treasurer, assessor, superintendent of the educational service region, state's attorney, recorder of deeds, and clerk of the court.

Townships

In eighty-four of Illinois' 102 counties, the land within the county is subdivided into townships, each of which has its own government. The township is grassroots government, the government closest to the people in rural areas. The township is also a basic unit for political party organization in Illinois.

Elected township officials include the members of the board of trustees, the township supervisor, an assessor, and a collector. These officers are elected for four-year terms.

Jon Randolph

Elgin is a municipality that grew up along the Fox River and now has a downtown mall with a government campus complex at riverside. Elgin, population 77,010, is a home rule city and has a city manager form of government with a mayor and seven council members elected every four years.

Frank Bell, Illiopolis Sentinel

As a snowstorm approaches in late winter of 1991, Illiopolis Township Highway Commissioner Les Havener (on grader) and his assistant, Jack Fenton, get ready to clear fifty-two miles of township roads in Sangamon County. In the summer, they will use the same equipment to repair the roads.

Townships have three primary functions: township roads, help to the needy, and assessing the value of local property for tax purposes. Through the supervisor, the township may also provide other social services, such as child care, job training, housing improvement, and health care which may include a drug abuse program. These social services have become increasingly important in the townships surrounding Chicago.

Municipalities

Besides the county and township governments, there are 1,274 municipalities in Illinois. Municipalities are also called cities, villages, and incorporated towns. (Do not confuse a small town with township govern-

Photos by Terry Farmer / Showcase Photography

At left is the center square in Winchester with a statue of Stephen A. Douglas, who lived and taught school in Winchester and whom Abraham Lincoln debated when both ran for the U.S. Senate in 1858. The city of Winchester, population 1,769, has an aldermanic form of government with a mayor and six aldermen. At right is the Elsah Village Hall. Elsah, a village of 851 people, is tucked away among the bluffs on Route 100, the Great River Road that parallels the Mississippi River for several miles.

ment.) Municipalities are independent government structures; they are not a part of either the county or township governments which serve the same area. Municipalities are usually formed when local residents petition the state to establish a city, a village, or an incorporated town because they want more services (such as city water or sewers) that are not provided by counties or townships.

Municipalities are located where people needed them; they were not set up by any master plan. Each municipality has its own reason or reasons for attracting people — a good river or lake port, a good rail location for shipping grain or other goods, a college, a bustling crossroads with stores and services set up to supply farmers who had settled on Illinois' rich prairie land. There are other reasons today, but all have to do with earning a good living. Municipalities were established to help serve the people attracted to these places.

Forms of Municipal Government

There are several forms of city government possible in Illinois: aldermanic, city manager, commission, and strong mayor. Villages may be organized under either the city manager form or a variation of the aldermanic form. Each has its own advantages and disadvantages as well as variations.

Aldermanic Form

The vast majority of Illinois' cities have an aldermanic form of government. Also called the "weak mayor-council form," it works well in smaller municipalities. It is called weak mayor-council because, under state law, the mayor's administrative powers are shared with the council. Of course, that doesn't mean that the mayor may not be a strong personality with great leadership ability. A succession of Chicago mayors, such as Richard J. Daley and Harold Washington, illustrates that the term "weak mayor" is organizational, not personal. In fact, many of the aldermanic communities throughout the state elect mayors who are strong political and governmental leaders.

These cities are known as aldermanic because, in most cases, the members of their city councils — their legislative bodies — are elected from wards, or districts, within the city. Sometimes two aldermen are elected from each district; in other cities, only one is elected per district. In most cities, the aldermen serve a four-year term of office; in a few cities, the term is only two years. The council makes policy, passes ordinances, and decides how the city's services will be managed.

While this form of government is used primarily in smaller cities, some larger ones use it, including Berwyn, Danville, East St. Louis, and Waukegan.

Village of Skokie

The Village of Skokie has a modern-day village hall, and its courtyard is shown in this photograph. The village is not a small town, however. With a population of 59,432, Skokie has home rule and a city manager form of government.

City Manager Form

The city manager form is like the aldermanic form: Voters elect a mayor and members of the city council. The council members may be elected from wards or districts within the city; they may be elected at-large (citywide); or some council members may be elected at-large while others are elected from wards. The terms and voting powers of the mayor and council members are the same as those in the aldermanic form.

The unique part of this form is that the mayor and council hire a professional administrator — usually someone trained in the management of city government. The city manager runs the daily business of the government. The mayor and council hire the person they feel is best for the city manager job and replace him or her when they wish. It is the job of the city manager to supervise everyone else working for the city, whether they buy toilet paper for city hall, keep police squad cars in repair, or trim trees on city property. The manager hires, fires, and supervises city workers.

The city manager also advises the council on how to improve the city. He or she may be called on to work out agreements with other cities on mutual problems such as waste disposal, new water supplies, or flooding. While doing all this, the manager is expected to keep costs low.

Most of Illinois' larger suburbs around Chicago and the larger cities downstate now use the city manager form. This includes, for example, the suburban communities around Chicago of Elgin, Elmhurst, Evanston, Joliet, Oak Park, and Skokie, as well as the central and southern Illinois cities of Bloomington, Carbondale, Champaign, Collinsville, Decatur, Galesburg, Mount Vernon, Peoria, Rock Island, and Urbana.

The Commission Form

In this form of government, voters elect a mayor and four commissioners on an at-large basis. Together these five people serve as the legislative body for local lawmaking. Each commissioner also is the administrative head of one of the city's departments, such as finance or public works. The council appoints a clerk and a treasurer. Once very popular, the commission form of government is now used in only twenty-one of the 389 Illinois cities and villages with populations over 2,500. Many people consider this form obsolete.

In both Springfield and Danville the federal courts threw out the commission form of government because the at-large elections never resulted in election of an African-American commissioner. To guarantee representation of this minority of citizens, these cities now have wards.

Strong Mayor-Council

Illinois law permits cities to choose a strong-mayor form of government. In this form the mayor, by law, becomes the chief executive officer, who is in charge of the work of all the administrative departments. The council's role is to make policy and pass ordinances. In this form, too, the mayor appoints a professional admin-

David K. Fremon

Hegewisch is a neighborhood in Chicago on the south side near Lake Calumet. Before being annexed by the city of Chicago in 1889, Hegewisch was organized as a company town, much like Pullman, to be a self-sustaining community for the work force of Adolph Hegewisch's steel mill. A decision by government for a proposed new third airport for Chicago could mean that Hegewisch will be replaced by a runway for the new airport.

David K. Fremon

This is the center of Chicago's Uptown neighborhood, at Wilson and Broadway where the elevated train makes its stop. Much of Chicago is connected via its subway and elevated train system, operated by the Chicago Transit Authority, a separate government authority (four members are appointed by the mayor of Chicago and three by the governor).

istrator to help supervise city employees. No Illinois city has adopted this option by vote of the people in a referendum, but at least three Illinois cities, however, do use a modified version of the strong-mayor form. Rockford and Aurora adopted many elements by ordinance; Springfield adopted this form in response to a court mandate that it drop the commission form.

Village Government

Village governments in Illinois are organized much like the city aldermanic form, except that the members of the village board, called trustees, are elected by the voters at-large, rather than by voters in wards. The powers of the village board are similar to those of the city council in the aldermanic form. The office of the village president is almost the same as the mayor in aldermanic cities.

Some village governments have chosen to use managers like the city manager form of government. They have either adopted the city manager form set out by state law, or they have passed an ordinance establishing the job of "village administrator."

Many people think of cities as large governments and villages as small governments, but there is no law that says so. The village of Skokie, for example, with a 1990 population of 59,432 likes to advertise itself as "the world's largest village." The city of Leland Grove has 1,679 people.

Chicago City Government

The government of the city of Chicago is based on the weak mayor-council model. The elected officials include the mayor, who is elected at-large, and a city council consisting of aldermen elected from fifty wards (one per ward). The city clerk and treasurer are also elected.

The mayor is the chief executive officer who appoints administrative staff for the twenty-four boards and commissions funded directly by the city. There are more than one hundred boards, commissions, and advisory groups. Most of their members are appointed by the mayor and approved by the council. Members of the boards of otherwise independent agencies, such as the Board of Education, the City Colleges, the Chicago Housing Authority, and the Chicago Transit Authority, are appointed in this fashion, too.

The mayor presides at city council meetings and can vote in the case of a tie. The mayor must approve or veto all ordinances passed by the city council. It is the Democratic Party primary that usually determines who

The State Journal-Register

will be Chicago's mayor because the winner of the Democratic primary has won the mayoral election for the past sixty years.

The Chicago City Council is composed of fifty aldermen (all officially called aldermen by law regardless of gender). Each alderman represents a ward of about 60,000 people and serves a four-year term. Aldermen are elected on a nonpartisan ballot at the same time as the mayoral primary (in February). If no candidate receives a majority in the regular election in a particular ward, there is a runoff election in April between the two candidates with the most votes. Even though the aldermanic elections have nonpartisan ballots, most people know to which political party the candidate belongs.

An alderman may or may not also be a ward committeeman. Each ward may have two committeemen — one Republican and one Democrat — who represent their party in the ward. The position of committeeman is an unpaid, elective party office separate from the aldermanic position, yet often the Democratic committeeman is very influential in Chicago's city government.

Local Government Powers

Local governments have only those powers given them by the state. They can exercise only the powers specified for them in either the state Constitution or in state statutes. For most local governments, such powers are quite limited. They can get more powers only by going to the state legislature to ask for them.

Some municipalities and counties have broader powers. These are given to them in the home rule provisions of the 1970 state Constitution. Governments which qualify for home rule can exercise any local powers not denied to them by state law or the Constitution. Home rule means the local government has broad power to control its own affairs.

Home rule powers have been used creatively by many municipalities to shift the burden of local taxes away from residents to nonresidents — from property taxes that residents pay to taxes on things like hotel rooms and amusements that nonresidents pay. Home rule is also widely used to lower the rate of interest that local governments pay on borrowed money.

All Illinois cities and villages with populations over 25,000 automatically have home rule unless voters specifically reject it in a referendum (a citywide vote). Smaller municipalities may adopt home rule by referendum. Counties acquire home rule powers by providing for an elected chief executive officer. Currently Cook County and over 100 municipalities have home rule.

Home rule is not unlimited. The Illinois Constitution puts limits on home rule powers and authorizes the General Assembly to do likewise. The drinking age

Bill Campbell

problem inspired one limit to home rule powers. Different communities had used their home rule powers to establish different minimum drinking ages. Some set age nineteen; others set age twenty-one. Highway accidents increased as youths drove to communities where they could legally drink. Enforcing such a confused variety of laws became chaotic. The General Assembly passed a law, taking away the home rule power to set drinking ages, leaving one minimum drinking age for all of Illinois as set by state law.

Special Districts: Schools

Of all the special districts, the best known are for schools. Illinois has 954 school districts, more than any other state except Texas and California. Illinois also has three types of school districts: 424 "unit" districts teach all grades; 416 "elementary" districts have only elemen-

Dick Paulus

tary and middle or junior high schools; and 114 "secondary" districts have only high schools. Because there are so many districts, the state encourages consolidation, which is the combining of two or more districts into one.

Every school district (except Chicago) elects citizens to serve as the school board. The board sets policy for its schools on curriculum and textbooks, it hires and fires the school superintendent, it establishes the school budget, and it levies local property taxes to help pay for schools. The superintendent is the chief administrative officer. He or she is responsible for hiring teachers and other staff, supervising the educational programs, and carrying out the policy decisions made by the school board within general requirements of state law.

The State Journal-Register

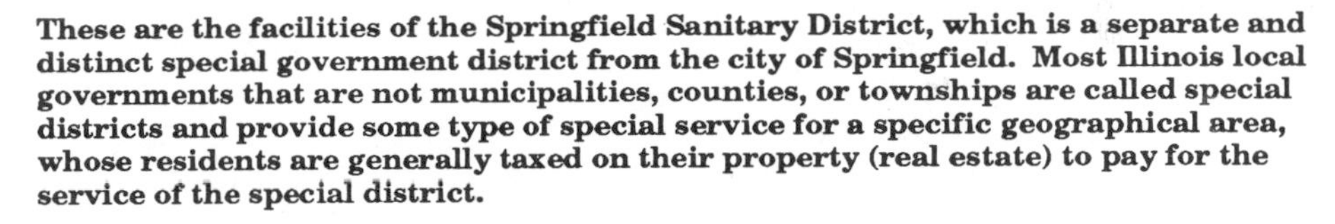

These are the facilities of the Springfield Sanitary District, which is a separate and distinct special government district from the city of Springfield. Most Illinois local governments that are not municipalities, counties, or townships are called special districts and provide some type of special service for a specific geographical area, whose residents are generally taxed on their property (real estate) to pay for the service of the special district.

Chicago Public Schools

Chicago's school system has had some of the greatest difficulties of any system in the state or nation. Problems stem from size, lack of money, and the challenge of teaching students from so many different backgrounds, including many from very disadvantaged backgrounds. In 1988 the General Assembly passed legislation to change how power is shared in the Chicago schools. The new law set up local school councils (one for each Chicago school), consisting of the principal of the school and ten elected members: six parents elected by parents, two community residents elected by community residents, and two teachers elected by school staff. In the high schools students elected a nonvoting member. These councils were given the power to approve the local school budget and thus determine the school's priorities and to choose its school's principal and develop a three-year school improvement plan.

In November 1990, the Illinois Supreme Court said the state law setting up the local school councils was unconstitutional because the members were not elected in a way that guaranteed representation to all citizens (one man, one vote). In January 1991, the General Assembly passed a new law to allow the school councils to continue by having all council members appointed by the mayor of Chicago. That law overcame the court ruling on the constitutional question, but the General Assembly was expected to consider more legislation in the spring of 1991 to assure that the local school councils will represent individual school interests.

Other Special Districts

Besides school districts, Illinois has about 3,000 other special district governments. Once you become a property tax payer, you will become aware of these special districts because they show up on your property tax bill: Each levies its separate tax within its district boundaries.

Each special district deals with a particular problem and provides a particular public service. Why does Illinois have so many of them? Some were created to provide services on a regional basis; others to provide services which existing governments could not afford. Still others were established to provide services that existing local governments cannot provide. County governments, for example, are not permitted by state law to have fire departments. Thus many people in rural areas established special fire protection districts to provide themselves with local fire protection services.

The largest number of special districts are for drainage and flood control, fire protection, parks and recreation, and sewerage. All of these districts serve important purposes, yet there are problems. Boundary lines are rarely the same for different kinds of governments serving the same area. Responsibility for local services is divided among so many boards that citizens became confused. As a result, citizens do not understand which government does what, and they frequently blame their city or county governments for tax increases imposed by

Terry Farmer / Showcase Photography

Many of Illinois' largest cities have mass transit districts, which are an example of special districts providing a specific service to a specific area. The bus pictured here is one of the fleet of the Springfield Mass Transit District, which is run by a five-member board appointed by the Sangamon County Board.

the boards of special districts. Also as a result, such special district boards often can and do raise taxes free of public resistance. The final result of so many special districts can be higher local property taxes.

Because there are so many special districts, citizens in Illinois have a greater opportunity to take part in local government than citizens in most other states. Each special district has its own governing board made up of local citizens. In some districts, these board members are elected; in others they are appointed by the local city council or county board. Usually each special district board appoints a chief executive officer to oversee the day-to-day functions of the district in much the same manner as the city manager does in a city.

Influences on Local Government

Everyone has an interest in influencing local government because local government affects everyone where they live. Local government tries to solve our everyday problems, including broken streetlights, potholes, or the need for a plan to get rid of garbage. People who call their city's aldermen or their county's board members with a complaint can be influencing government decisions. Government decisions are also influenced by organized citizens or interest groups. They pressure city councils, county boards, and other local government officials through organized campaigns. Unlike the state and federal government the decision-makers of local government are easy to reach, and citizens have a greater chance to influence them, especially if they organize as a group.

Not only do local citizens reach up to influence their local governments, but higher levels of government reach down to influence local affairs. Funds provided by state and federal grants for particular services, such as welfare or roads, make a difference in local decision-making. There are also cooperative local governmental planning bodies, such as the Northeastern Illinois Planning Commission, often referred to as NIPC (pronounced NIP-see).

Overlapping Local Governments

Especially complicated are the decision-making relationships between governments serving the same geographic area, such as townships, villages, counties, and school districts. People living in the city of De Kalb, for instance, are served by the city, by De Kalb County, by De Kalb Unit School District, by De Kalb Township, and by the De Kalb Sanitary District. The boundaries of all of these governments are not the same. The school district boundaries include land outside the city limits; the city's boundaries include De Kalb Township, but also parts of several other townships.

This duplication of government in one geographic area leads to questions of who is responsible for providing what service. De Kalb, for instance, is served by four

The State Journal-Register / Sangamon Valley Collection, Lincoln Library

In 1987 blacks opposing a voting rights lawsuit settlement with the city of Springfield demonstrated against a "fairness hearing" concerning the proposed agreement between the plaintiffs and city officials. Federal Judge Harold Baker ruled against the protestors and let stand the original settlement, which called for a strong-mayor form of government with aldermen elected from wards.

The State Journal-Register

law enforcement agencies: the city police, the county sheriff's department, the Northern Illinois University campus police, and the State Police. One day, when students blocked a state highway in the middle of a campus demonstration, the four police departments met in the middle of the street and argued about which department was in charge and responsible for dealing with the students.

Issues about which government is responsible are common: Who provides police protection to a school district with borders overlapping county and village boundaries? Does the city health department have control of the way food is served in the school district cafeteria? Sometimes such disputes over government responsibility have to be settled in court. Such issues do not abide the boundaries of government.

Interest Groups

Interest groups try to influence the decisions of every kind and form of local government. Such groups include a chamber of commerce looking for favorable business conditions, like better parking for customers. They include neighborhood groups seeking to improve parks or police protection or the enforcement of building codes; taxpayer groups concerned about high taxes; humanitarian groups trying to have government solve homelessness; and citizens like you looking for a place to skateboard.

Interest groups may be small and informal or large and very well-organized. People may band together to deal with one special problem such as the need for a traffic light at a busy intersection. Once the local government responds to that problem, this type of group may dissolve. Another group formed to see that the local park is kept clean may continue as a group for years to keep the pressure constantly on government.

Political parties may also have major influence on local government. Many municipalities have sought to reduce the pressures of national and state politics on local matters through nonpartisan elections. In a nonpartisan election candidates for mayor or alderman are not listed with a party label on the voting ballot. The candidates may or may not be members of the Democratic or Republican parties, but they are not officially identified with either for the local election. Sometimes citizens will develop local parties with names such as Citizen's Caucus or Citizen's Party in order to find and support qualified candidates for local government offices. Such local parties may be listed on ballots in some communities.

In general, national political parties, Republican or Democratic, do not have much influence on local government except in the larger cities and in counties and townships. Most municipalities and school districts operate much differently, with little party influence and with people appointed to government jobs on the basis of merit, rather than party activity.

Media

Another powerful influence on local government is the local media. If there is a local newspaper, television, or radio station, the opinions of the people controlling those media are very important to government. Often there are few sources of information in a community. The news of a village council as reported or not reported by a local newspaper or radio station makes a big difference in the way people think about the council's decisions.

If, for example, the local newspaper reports that garbage is piling up in backyards and the council is ignoring the problem, the citizens will probably become angry. If a particular local business is given a contract to provide supplies for city hall and no other businesses are allowed to compete for the business, the news media should report this unfairness to the public. If no one asks or reports the situation to the community, nothing will change. The media play a major role in keeping people informed and in influencing the opinion the people have of their government.

Citizens must be careful, however, not to rely solely on the local news media for information about government. Members of the media can and do make mistakes; information in the newspaper or on the radio or TV can be wrong. In the above example of the business contract, the newspaper might not report the story if the businessman is an advertiser in the newspaper and the paper's publisher does not want to risk losing his business. Thus, citizens need always to remain alert for information about their governments.

A Modern Problem and Pressures: Developers

In recent years certain business men and women called developers have become major interest groups pressuring municipalities and counties of every size. Developers are in the business of combining land and buildings for a particular use, like a shopping mall. Their plans for land and buildings are called "developments." The land may or may not already have buildings on it. Developments include such things as subdivisions of private homes, groups of apartment buildings, industrial parks, and large or small shopping centers.

Developers need local government help to provide public services such as water, sewer, and police and fire protection to their new developments. They also need cooperation on such city regulations as parking, land use, construction permits, or taxation. Because the developers want to make a profit from their finished developments, they will try very hard to get governments to provide such services and to cooperate on local regulations. Developers try to convince officials of the "good" things their development will bring to the community: more jobs, more tax revenue for government services, and attractive new or renovated facilities. Developments are often opposed, however, because they can increase traffic, put pressure on municipal services, reduce the amount of open space, cause architecturally interesting and historic buildings to be torn down, or cause pollution. The arguments can be intense, making it hard for local officials to decide what is best. Developers are often far better organized and prepared with information than either local governments or citizens' groups.

Developers as a special interest group are growing in influence. Some local governments, especially in rapidly expanding areas, face decisions on developments every day. Other communities have little to attract developers and might actually welcome the challenge of dealing with them.

The Voters' Influence

The citizens themselves are an important influence in any local government. As voters, they elect government leaders, and leaders who fail to be sensitive to the wishes of the voters may not get reelected to office.

There are also times when the elected representatives, like a city council or school district board, do not have the power to make decisions for the people. Instead, all the voters get to decide. The device for everyone to vote on a question is called a referendum. A referendum may be required for increasing taxes, going into debt, changing the form of government, or getting (or getting rid of) home rule. All these referenda are binding, meaning the decision of the voters must be followed. There are also advisory or nonbinding referenda that let local officials know how the citizens feel about an issue.

Economic Pressures

Economic pressures influence the decisions of local government. Remember that people move or stay because of jobs. Some Illinois communities, especially those in counties surrounding Chicago, are experiencing rapid growth. Business is booming and people are moving there. Governments there must deal with needs for new facilities for water, sewerage, transportation, and local shopping. For other communities in Illinois, growth has slowed or stopped altogether because their major industries have gotten into trouble. Governments in such cities as Rock Island, Peoria, Decatur, and Cairo must deal with ways of attracting new jobs or helping their existing businesses to expand.

Who's in Charge?

What happens when a community has a problem to solve? How do the complexities of local government influence the way a problem is solved?

As you can tell, local government, with its many kinds and forms, is complex. Finding out exactly who is responsible can be as confusing as finding your way through a maze or a video game screen. Consider these different issues: If a school lies outside a municipality or between two municipalities, who provides police protection since school districts do not have police forces? The courts have decided that a municipality within one mile of the school must take responsibility. Can a county government inspect a school cafeteria for health standards? The Illinois attorney general has ruled that it can. The court decision and attorney general's opinion are two ways for dealing with the confusion.

But, more often, the confusion is settled, and public policy decisions are made, through long, time-consuming processes of negotiation between the governments involved, private citizens with a special interest in the matter, affected interest groups, and sometimes the agencies of federal and state governments. When many different governments work together to solve a problem, the process is called intergovernmental relations.

Much of the work of local government, and indeed much of the work of all governments, is accomplished through different government agencies working together. This process is described in more detail in the opening section of the next chapter.

CHAPTER 8

The Way It Works

By Darlene Emmert Fisher, Michael D. Klemens, Eleanor Meyer, and Patrick J. Burns

Government today — whether it be the national government in Washington, D.C., Illinois' state government in Springfield, or one of the local governments serving your community — is a big and complex business. Government faces tough and complex problems. Even the question of where you can go to use your skateboard is a hard problem. The government must be sure that the place selected does not have other people who might be hit and hurt by skateboarders; that the place will not have any features, such as rocks or steep hills, that might increase the chances that skateboarders will be hurt. Any place selected must be easy for kids to get to by bike or on foot. Then the possible opposition of persons who own or use the surrounding land must be considered. The final question is one of the toughest: What sort of insurance protection can be provided to protect everyone involved from lawsuits resulting from any injuries caused by skateboarding?

Government has no easy problems, and so there are no easy answers to any of them. Most involve some effort on the part of several different government agencies. This is called intergovernmental relations. All involve the expenditure of money — of the tax money which we all pay. All, too, involve political activity by citizens who are interested and concerned with the decisions their government is making.

These three — intergovernmental relations, tax dollars, and citizen input — are the ingredients of government activity. They are the subject of this last chapter which ties together much of what you have learned in this book and shows you how the business of government is done and how it raises and spends money. The last section of this chapter is perhaps the most important of all: It explains how you can make your government work for you!

**Top photo of garbage by The State Journal-Register.
Middle photo of Old Orchard Mall courtesy of the Village of Skokie.
Bottom photo of state Sen. Walter Dudycz in 1989 leading a demonstration in front of the Art Institute of Chicago.**

**Section 1
Intergovernmental Relations: A Case Study**

**Section 2
Finances: A Day at the Mall**

**Section 3
Citizen Involvement: It Is Your Choice**

Section 1
Intergovernmental Relations: A Case Study
By Darlene Emmert Fisher

Most problems that government must solve involve intergovernmental relations. That means that not one agency resolves a problem. Instead, it takes the cooperative action by many different agencies of government, each concerned with a different part of the problem.

To explain how intergovernmental relations works, let's look at one of our state's and nation's real problems — garbage.

Case Study: Getting Rid of the Garbage

It used to be easy to throw away garbage. All you had to do was find some vacant land away from houses, toss garbage on it, and you had a garbage dump. Today it is not so easy. Now we know that dumps attract rats, produce foul odors, create litter, and pollute the earth and the water that lies under the ground.

Even worse, there is not much vacant land left near our cities, and the dumps that we do have are filling up. Our society is now producing record amounts of garbage to get rid of. Every man, woman, and child generate a massive amount of garbage each year. Each American contributes 3.6 pounds per day to the problem, and, in an industrial city like Chicago, the total reaches five pounds a day. Most of us don't want that trash in our backyard or in our neighborhood.

Even recycling the glass, aluminum cans, and other materials in our garbage into new bottles, cans, and other products does not solve the problem. In Illinois, in 1989, approximately four or five percent of our garbage was being recycled compared with two percent in 1987. That is an improvement but still leaves ninety-five percent to be stashed in dumps, or what we now call landfills.

But our landfills are almost filled up, and Illinois state law says new ones can only be opened if local residents agree. Local residents say "No" because they fear the dangers of poisonous trash, the threat to underground supplies of drinking water, and the heavy truck traffic of garbage haulers. Thus, management of our garbage and other waste is a major issue of modern society.

The problem involves many different governments. Townships, especially in rural areas, often provide dumping locations. Because cities, villages, and counties are responsible for the health and welfare of their citizens, they must find ways to get rid of the garbage their citizens produce. These governments must also protect their residents and their land, water, and air from the pollution that landfills can create. Finally, they must deal with the pressure from their local residents who want to get rid of their garbage but don't want landfills in their neighborhood. The issue of sites for landfills has been identified by political scientists as one of our "NIMBY" problems: Everyone wants their trash hauled someplace, but "Not In My Back Yard."

State government is also concerned with protection

The State Journal-Register

This unsightly and unhealthy garbage was dumped illegally in a secluded wooded area. State laws and local ordinances regulate the disposal of garbage.

The State Journal-Register

X-L Recycling in Crestwood processes 100 percent and recycles 70-75 percent of household garbage dumped at stations like this one.

A recycling drop-off site at Sangamon Center North Shopping Center in Springfield takes aluminum cans, glass, and newspaper. Springfield does not operate garbage pick-up or recycling as a municipal service. Instead, private companies operate garbage pick-up services, charging fees to their customers. Private companies also operate recycling businesses. When cities mandate recycling and the cost of picking up recyclable items is greater than their market value, the losses are passed on by the disposal companies to their customers.

The State Journal-Register

of the environment from dangerous waste. The Illinois Environmental Protection Agency has established standards for potential problem areas like landfills, trash dumps, and factory waste disposal. The state park system must protect its parks from trash. The Department of Nuclear Safety is concerned with the disposal of low-level nuclear waste. The Illinois Geological Survey and Illinois Water Survey are concerned with landfill sites because of the effect of trash and seepage in sand, earth, rock formations, and underground water supplies.

At the federal level, there is another Environmental Protection Agency establishing national standards regarding tolerable amounts of environmental damage. The federal agency executes the laws passed by Congress. Special legislation protects particular areas such as wetlands, which often seem to be wasteland to local farmers and developers and yet are important parts of the ecological system and are vital to sustaining forms of wildlife and controlling some flooding problems. The U.S. Army Corps of Engineers is charged with oversight of river and lake projects on the nation's waterways and has a responsibility to protect waterways from pollution.

Illinois Department of Conservation

A wetlands area in southern Illinois is a popular resting place for Canada geese. In 1991 Illinois had 920,000 acres of natural wetlands. In 1818, when Illinois became a state, there were 8.2 million acres of wetlands. In 163 years Illinois lost ninety percent of its wetland resources.

The State Journal-Register

The Sangamon Valley Landfill is located left of center where the mound rises out of the trees. The city of Springfield is in the background and the Sangamon River is in the foreground, less than a mile away from the disposal site. Landfills throughout Illinois are filling up, and citizens often do not want new ones to open near where they live.

What to Do about It

What is a community to do about its garbage? State law now requires that all counties and the city of Chicago develop waste management programs, including recycling. State law also prohibits putting yard waste, such as grass clippings and leaves, in landfills. The state now has a tax on garbage hauled to landfills, and the proceeds from that tax help communities start recycling programs. But there is still a lot of garbage to be disposed of, and we are running out of places to put it.

Take the case of the Northwest Municipal Conference, an organization of thirty-one suburbs in Cook County. The conference planned to take responsibility for all the waste produced by its member communities, so it proposed to set up a "balefill," a disposal area where compressed packages of waste would be deposited.

The conference chose a site in an isolated area for the balefill and set up a new, special district unit of government called the Solid Waste Agency of Northern Cook County (SWANCC). The agency established a goal of seventy percent reduction in volume of waste before it is disposed of (forty percent recycyling, five percent source reduction, twenty-five percent baling for volume reduction). Waste reduction and recycling are integral to the plan. Twenty-six of the conference's members joined the new agency and planned to use the proposed balefill. Significantly, none of the communities near the proposed site joined the new government agency or planned to use the balefill to dispose of their garbage. The communities which joined SWANCC were all located five to forty miles from the proposed balefill site.

Opposition to the proposed location for the balefill came immediately from residents and communities in the vicinity of the suggested site and from more distant communities concerned that the balefill would pollute underground drinking water supplies. Environmentalists were also concerned because the proposed site included one of the few remaining nesting sites for blue herons in the northern Illinois region.

In a situation like this, a small number of angry opponents may have a dramatic influence. Governmental boards, especially those at the local level, are accustomed to very limited citizen interest in their work. The very vocal and sometimes dramatic protests of even a small group of people may be very influential at these board meetings. Local officials, especially, do not like to be unpopular with their neighbors. Their reluctance to act on even urgent problems in the face of NIMBY opposition has led to another phenomenon, "NIMTO" (Not In My Term of Office), in which problems are simply postponed by government officials because no one wants to deal with them.

Dick Paulus

The Decision Process

Once the SWANCC decided to proceed with its balefill plan, the agency first went to the village of Bartlett for annexation and local siting approval, but the village refused both. Next SWANCC took its proposal to the Cook County government for zoning approval. Despite strong protests from officials in adjacent communities and from citizens groups, the Cook County Board gave preliminary approval to the plan, but only after developing a way to establish a one million dollar per year fund to guarantee the value of neighboring property and the safety of drinking water supplies.

Opposition then focused on the next step: the required approval from the Illinois Environmental Protection Agency. That agency originally found problems with groundwater monitoring at the site. Groundwater is important because the old gravel pit site of the balefill is above an underground water supply from which many communities pumped their drinking water. After changes in the plans were made to further protect the groundwater supplies, the Illinois Environmental Protection Agency did approve the balefill.

Next, the approval process went to the U.S. Army Corps of Engineers, which, according to SWANCC, at first did not claim jurisdiction. Since the proposed site fills with storm water runoff part of the year and serves as a habitat for migratory waterfowl, it came under the Corps' jurisdiction.

The problem was immediately complicated for the Corps by a U.S. congressman who opposed the balefill. He added an amendment to a congressional appropriation bill for funding the Corps: The amendment would require the Corps to consult with the U.S. Environmental Protection Agency and report to Congress about potential water problems.

Routine procedures require that the Corps hold a public hearing on the issue and solicit input from other affected government agencies. Among those which provided such input were the Illinois Department of Conservation, the Illinois Endangered Species Board, the U.S. Department of the Interior, the U.S. Environmental Protection Agency, and the federal agency concerned with migratory fowl and wildlife. Most recommended against the proposed balefill site.

If the decision is made to do a full environmental impact study, it will take a year or more to complete, and then the Corps could make its decision. The U.S. Environmental Protection Agency could also veto the site. In August 1990, those decisions were still pending.

Three Elements of Government Interaction

Three elements are important to note from this description of a real case of intergovernmental relations. First, the business of government is very complex. Even a simple question — where do I throw my garbage — is a hard question that can take years to answer. The answer must take into account not only your interest in getting rid of your garbage but the community's interest in protecting the purity of its drinking water, the interests of the landfill's neighbors in protecting their property values and preventing landscape littering and pollution, the concerns of those interested in the preservation of wildlife, and everyone who is concerned with keeping down the cost of garbage disposal.

The second element to note is the number of different government agencies: the thirty-one suburbs who are members of the Northwest Municipal Conference, the twenty-six joining the newly created special district (SWANCC), the municipalities who did not join, Cook County, several different agencies of the state of Illinois, several different agencies of the federal government, and even the U.S. Congress. All of these are a part of the answer to the simple question, "Where can I throw my garbage?"

Terry Farmer / Showcase Photography

Illinois has waterways to protect as sources of drinking water, as commercial transportation routes, and as recreational resources. The Illinois River is part of the main barge route from Chicago to New Orleans on the Gulf of Mexico. Above is a barge on the Illinois River where it flows into the Mississippi River at Grafton.

Illinois Department of Conservation

These great blue herons nesting in trees near the proposed balefill site in Cook County may have to find a new nesting area if the trees are cut down for the landfill.

Finally, each of the different agencies was not just an added layer of bureaucratic red tape, but a source for new ideas about how to prevent the landfill from harming anything or anyone. The Northwest Municipal Conference offered many suggestions to make the landfill an acceptable neighbor. The new, special district, SWANCC, was created. The opposition of other communities and groups led SWANCC and other government agencies to look harder for answers to their concerns. As a result, Cook County set up the fund to protect property values and drinking water; the Illinois Environmental Protection Agency forced improvements in the groundwater monitoring system and built in more safety measures; and the hearings before the U.S. Army Corps of Engineers have produced a proposal calling for SWANCC, which would manage the balefill, to create an artificial island with nesting sites for the blue herons during their annual mating season.

The input of each different government agency did not simply delay the project; this intergovernmental process helped to make the proposed solution to the garbage problem a better solution, a solution that will do more to protect the public's health and the quality of the environment.

Section 2

Finances: A Day at the Mall

By Michael D. Klemens

It's one of those blustery March days that isn't good for much. It's too muddy to play ball and too cold to hang around the park. Your dad or your mom's sitting at the kitchen table with a calculator and a stack of papers grumbling about this receipt or that check and complaining about taxes. "I'm doing the taxes," you're told. It does not look like fun.

Clearly it's not a day to hang around the house. So you call up Eddie — he's got his driver's license and his mom lets him take the car — and propose a trip to the mall. Anything to get away from those taxes. But you can't get away from taxes. Everybody pays them, even teenagers who hang around the mall on early spring Saturdays. Let's keep an eye on the taxes paid in an afternoon at the mall.

Eddie arrives forty-five minutes later with Rob and Jeff. "I need gas you guys. Ante up." Gas is 99.9 cents a gallon, so a dollar apiece buys you three gallons. A good part of that dollar goes for taxes. Actually, three dollars gets you two dollars' worth of gasoline and pays one dollar in taxes to the federal, state, and local governments.

The State Journal-Register

Taxes on Gasoline

When you buy gasoline in Illinois, you pay two different kinds of state taxes: gasoline (the precise name is "motor fuel") taxes and sales taxes. To those who pay them, a tax is a tax; the difference comes in how the taxes are used. Motorists pay gasoline taxes on each gallon of gasoline they buy. The state uses some of this tax money to build and maintain highways. The state highway crew you see patching the road is probably paid with gasoline tax money. So is the crew building the new relief highway around the city, but less directly. When building new roads, the state usually borrows the money to build the roads by selling bonds, and then pays the money back to the bondholders with gasoline taxes. Finally, Illinois shares some of the money from its gasoline tax with local governments (cities, villages, counties, and townships), which use their portion to build new roads, fix potholes, and paint stripes on the highways.

Illinois Department of Transportation

Your tax money at work. Crews are repairing a stretch of Illinois Route 104 in Sangamon County between Auburn and Interstate 55. Each year, state workers use almost 33,000 tons of pothole patching material, nearly a half-million gallons of crack and joint sealer, and one-third billion tons of salt in maintaining the 42,762 lane miles of state highways.

Besides state gasoline taxes, most Illinoisans also pay local gasoline taxes. Local taxes on gasoline also pay for roads. In Chicago total local gasoline taxes are eleven cents per gallon. In Cook County outside Chicago, they are six cents per gallon. In Du Page County, they are four cents per gallon. Six other cities impose one cent per gallon gasoline taxes.

The other tax that you pay when you buy gasoline in Illinois is the sales tax. Sales taxes are charged for the purchase of goods and for a few services. When you buy a dollar's worth of gasoline, you will pay state sales taxes of 6.25 cents. You will also pay some local sales taxes in most places in Illinois. Local sales taxes, for example,

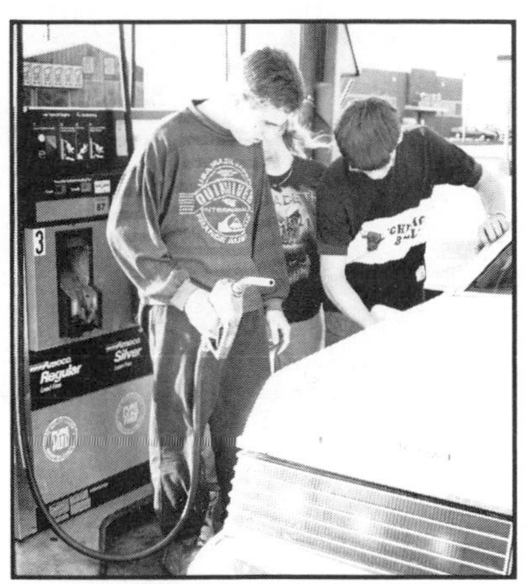

Terry Farmer / Showcase Photography

Taxes on gasoline.

help pay the cost of operating mass transit systems in and around Chicago and in Illinois across from St. Louis.

Although a tax is a tax, the difference between gasoline and sales taxes is how they are used. The state sales tax is the single largest state source of money that it uses for general operating expenses. That means the sales tax is used for things like running schools and public universities, operating prisons, paying welfare grants, providing mental hospitals, and investigating child abuse.

That is a long-winded explanation. As you pump your three dollars' worth into the tank, the numbers just turn round on the pump, without distinguishing between the price of gasoline and the taxes on gasoline.

Sales Taxes

You arrive at the mall and inside is an auto show. New car dealers are showing their wares. A Porsche catches your eye. Price: $22,495, plus tax. Rob growls that he could probably buy a used car with the tax on the Porsche. He's right; the state sales tax on the Porsche would be nearly $1,500. And then he would have to pay to register the car (buy license plates), a $48 charge that would seem pretty insignificant on a new car.

More taxes. It's enough to make a guy thirsty. Run in and buy a soda, and you'll run into more taxes. You're going to pay sales tax on that soda, a burger, or french fries. Buy a pair of jeans or a new T-shirt, and you'll pay sales tax. How about the newest tape from your favorite heavy metal group? More sales taxes.

Is nothing sacred? Is there no place to escape taxes? You could go watch a movie. As of now there is no sales tax on tickets to the movies in most Illinois communities. Nor is there a tax on what you pay a barber or a beautician, a lawyer, or a doctor. You may be able to buy tickets to a ball game or a rock concert without paying a tax. But if you want to buy the tape of a concert at a music store, expect to pay sales tax.

How about groceries? Surely government would not tax the food on a family's table. Sorry, you are wrong again, although you have hit at one of the touchy points of the state's tax system. Between 1980 and 1984 the state phased out most of the sales tax on food and medicine. You are still going to pay a one percent sales

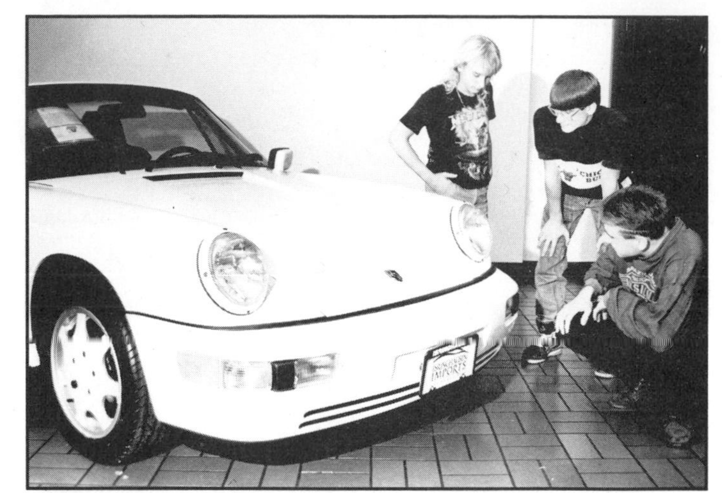

Taxes on automobiles.

Taxes on music and videotapes.

Photos by Terry Farmer / Showcase Photography

No taxes (usually) on movie tickets.

tax on groceries and medicine, but that tax money ends up in the hands of city and county governments, not the state government treasury.

State government taxes other necessities, like electricity, natural gas, and telephone calls. The maximum tax in each case is five percent. And local governments have the option of imposing their own utility taxes, too.

Income Taxes

But if you really want to understand taxes, you ought to get a job. Once you are working and earning money, you really begin to pay taxes. Get a job pushing burgers at the local fast food joint for four dollars an hour, fifteen hours per week. Imagine that in one year, between January 1 and December 31, you work fifty weeks. You would have $3,000 to spend or save, right?

Wrong. You have to pay income taxes on what you make. We're talking about state taxes in this book, so we'll concentrate on the Illinois state income tax. There is a federal income tax on what you earn, too. Fortunately, the Illinois income tax form is simpler to complete than the federal form.

Here's how it works. The state of Illinois, like most states that levy an income tax, is pretty clever. It takes its share of the income tax before you are paid. So from your first $60 paycheck (we'll assume you are paid weekly) it would keep $1.50. This practice is called withholding, and under it your employer takes a certain percentage of your salary and ships it off to the Illinois Department of Revenue. This does two things. It saves you from having to make a big tax payment at the end of the year, when you might not have the money or income on a steady basis. It also ensures that the state gets its money. You can decide which is the more important reason.

Also withheld from your paycheck are federal income taxes. Your employer sends that money to the U.S. Treasury. And social security taxes are also taken out of your pay. That money goes to the U.S. Social Security Administration, which uses the money to make social security payments to retired persons. Although today you might prefer to see the cash, the fact that you have made social security contributions will someday entitle you to retirement benefits.

Anyway, let's imagine that this goes on all year. Fifty paychecks means fifty $1.50 withholdings that go to the state, or total payments of $75. Sometime the following January your employer will give you a form — about one-third the size of this page — that shows how much you made and how much was withheld for state and federal taxes. These "W-2" forms will have carbon copies attached, so you can send copies with your federal and state income tax forms.

Illinois lets its citizens earn $1,000 without having

Dick Paulus

to pay any income tax. The $1,000 is called the "personal exemption." If you earn more than $1,000, you are required by law to fill out and mail to the Illinois Department of Revenue a state income tax form. Even if you do not earn $1,000, you probably should fill out the form anyway because most young people are entitled to an income tax refund. That means that you may be able to get back some of the $75 that you earned but was "withheld" from your paycheck.

The Illinois income tax form, named the IL-1040, is a single page and, compared with the federal form, is simple. If you had $3,000 in income, you are entitled to reduce that amount by the state personal exemption — the $1,000 that Illinois lets you earn without paying taxes. That leaves your taxable income at $2,000. If the

Illinois Department of Conservation

Fishing Illinois waters requires a license from the state, unless you are under sixteen or over sixty-four. Unlike driver's licenses, a fishing license issued in one state is not valid in another state. The Department of Conservation has its own enforcement division to make sure fishermen have a license.

income tax rate is three percent, you figure the taxes you owe at three percent of $2,000, or $60. (For those of us unable to do percentages, you can look up what you owe in taxes on a table printed inside the instruction booklet that comes with the form.)

The point here is that while $75 was withheld from your pay, you ended up owing only $60 in taxes. Fill out the tax form, mail it in, and the state will send you a check for $15. The same is probably true for your federal income tax, but you will not get back any of the social security taxes that you paid.

The Lottery

State government has other ways of raising money besides taxes. One of the best known is the Illinois state lottery. The best proof of the popularity of this state revenue source comes from the long lines of people waiting to buy lottery tickets whenever there is a big jackpot. Each year the lottery earns about half a billion dollars for Illinois, while returning another half billion dollars to winners. Although you hear a lot about the lottery, it is pretty small potatoes when compared to income and sales taxes, which each total about $4 billion per year. Lottery profits account for about five cents of every dollar that the state collects in taxes and fees.

The lottery is supposed to help schools. It does, but not as much as is claimed. Lottery profits all go to elementary and secondary schools, but because of the lottery money, education gets less other state money. It's kind of like trying to fill up a gallon pail with pennies. If you dump in a quart of lottery pennies, then you only need three quarts of other pennies. If you have no lottery pennies, you need four quarts of other pennies.

User Fees

State government also raises money with user fees. If you want to camp in a state park, you pay a camping fee. The state uses the money to maintain the park. If you want to go fishing (and you're sixteen or over), you buy a fishing license. The state uses the money from fishing licenses to run fish hatcheries to raise fish for you and others to catch. The garbage company pays a fee for each ton of waste dumped in landfills. Those fees are used to pay for recycling programs and to study ways to keep landfills from filling up so fast. And the garbage company, in turn, raises its price so that the person who throws away the garbage ends up paying. If your city has its own garbage trucks, the city will charge a fee or tax to cover the cost.

Note the relationship between the fee and what it is used for. Now you know where the term "user fee" comes from. The principle is that the person who is using the service should pay the fee. If I hate fish and cannot stand to handle worms, why should I pay taxes to raise fish for you to catch?

Dick Paulus

Taxes for Society in General

Other services benefit everyone. Public schools are an example. Long ago people decided that society benefited from having citizens who could read, write, and do mathematics. In theory, when the state spends money on schools, it is investing in its future — the young people who will hold the jobs and run the government. It would be pretty hard to make children or their parents come up with the $3,500 on average that is spent annually to educate each Illinois elementary and high school student. Likewise, the citizens of Illinois want to be safe in their homes. To accomplish this, the state and its cities and counties have police. Imagine how difficult it would be to charge a user fee for calling the police. The same is true of clean air and clean water. Everybody benefits from them and everybody pays part of the cost.

That is the principle of taxation. Everybody pays a little bit of the cost. The sales tax that you pay when you buy a new CD gets thrown in the hopper with the income taxes your teacher pays and with the profits from this week's Lotto drawing. In the ideal case, no one pays too much and everybody benefits. About one-third of the money that the state spends comes from the sales tax, and another one-third comes from the state income tax. The rest comes from an assortment of other taxes on things including gasoline, cigarettes, liquor, telephone calls, and horse racing bets.

How Your Tax Dollars Are Spent

In turn, those taxes get spent for a variety of things. About twenty-five cents of each dollar of state taxes gets spent on education — for elementary and high schools, public universities, and college financial aid. About twenty cents of each dollar gets spent on transportation, primarily roads and bridges but also airports, bus systems, and trains. About fifteen cents of each dollar is spent on various welfare programs, and ten cents of each dollar is spent for health and human services. Smaller amounts are spent on environmental protection, state police, and prison systems.

Too Many Taxes?

In the real world most people think they pay too many taxes. The late Maurice Scott, who served as president of the Taxpayers' Federation of Illinois, used to open talks by saying he had found the ideal tax. A tax on hair oil (an old-fashioned kind of styling gel). Mr. Scott nearly always got a laugh from the crowd when he said this because he was bald.

Because taxes are unpopular, politicians are wary about raising taxes. In 1969 Gov. Richard B. Ogilvie championed — and pushed through the General Assembly — the first income tax in Illinois. Three years later Ogilvie was defeated when he ran for reelection. Listen carefully to the political ads on the radio and television just before the next election. Invariably one candidate, sometimes both, will be trying to convince voters that his or her opponent is or will be guilty of raising taxes.

Too Few Services?

Although no one likes to pay more taxes, plenty of people want new or expanded services from government. Visit the state Capitol in June if you want to see who. Almost daily there are rallies by groups who want the state to start new programs or spend more money on what it already does. A group of homeless people may be camped on the lawn to illustrate the need for more money for housing. College students may be arguing for more state tax money for universities so that they do not have to pay higher tuition. Hospital workers may be demanding higher state payments for treating Illinoisans on welfare.

The people who want more services from state government often argue that state taxes in Illinois are low. They are right. The people who do not depend on state services often argue that in Illinois taxes are high. They are right, too. In Illinois the state taxes, particularly state income taxes, are low. However, taxes by local governments — cities, villages, counties, school districts, park districts, and all the other special local government districts — are high. The low state taxes and high local taxes balance off, leaving Illinois' tax burden at about the average for the United States.

Property Taxes: A Local Tax

In 1988 state and local governments in Illinois collected $1,782 in taxes for each person in Illinois. That was just about the average for the nation. State income taxes in 1988 averaged $272 per person, or about $110 below the U.S. average. But property taxes collected in 1988 averaged $628 per person in Illinois, about $90 above the average. Property taxes are based on the value of land and buildings, including homes, factories, stores, and farmland. Property taxes provide much of the money for public schools and for running the governments and providing the services of our cities, villages, counties, townships, and special districts. In short, state income taxes are low in Illinois, while local property taxes are high.

Elected officials often end up being torn between those who want more government services and those who want lower taxes. State legislators are elected to "do" things, and they like to bring projects home to their districts. Those projects include new roads and bridges, a new runway at the local air-

Illinois Department of Conservation

Illinois Department of Transportation

Taxes pay for many things. Projects such as the flood control work shown (at left) and the major upgrading of Chicago's Dan Ryan Expressway (at right) are obvious. Other projects are not so obvious. For example, the Department of Commerce and Community Affairs awarded a grant to X-L Recycling in Crestwood to implement technology that would separate from garbage various types of plastics, which can be recycled into new products and benefit the environment.

port, state money for a program to fight teen pregnancy, and new storm sewers for an area that is being flooded. Citizens want these services, but, at the same time, the same citizens as voters often object to new taxes.

'Bullfighting Arena' in Peoria

That dilemma produces another characteristic of state tax increases. They are apt to have a little something for everybody. Say, for example, that the city of Peoria decided to become the bullfighting capital of North America. Say also that the city leaders have made a convincing case that they could attract millions of tourists to Peoria if they had year-round bullfighting in a covered bullfighting arena. The tourists would occupy hotel rooms, eat in local restaurants, buy gasoline, and shop in the stores. All this activity would provide jobs for Peorians and new tax revenue for local and state governments.

The problem is that Peoria would need a covered bullfighting ring, a $200 million expense for which the city doesn't have the money. So it is proposed that the state will pay half the cost and raise that money through a one-cent increase in the cigarette tax. To provide the money for the Peoria bullfighting ring, state legislators must pass a law to raise the cigarette tax.

For the three legislators from Peoria — one state senator and two state representatives — that would be a pretty easy vote. Those three legislators could tell their constituents that they have to pay higher cigarette taxes to build this new facility. It is much more difficult for the other fifty-eight state senators and 116 state representatives. The higher cigarette taxes may anger voters in Chicago, Alton, and Urbana, who believe they are paying higher taxes but seeing no benefit. If they get mad enough, they may vote against their state legislators in the next election.

So it is unlikely that legislators will raise the state cigarette tax to build something for Peoria. Far more likely is the prospect that they would raise the cigarette tax five cents or ten cents and fund a series of projects across the state so Chicago might get a new hockey arena, Alton a dog racing track, Effingham a new stock car race track at the same time Peoria gets the bullfighting arena.

There has to be enough in the package to attract the votes needed to pass a tax increase in the General Assembly. For example, the temporary income tax increase of 1989 won passage in part because it provided more money to every school district and to every city, village, and county government in Illinois. Each legislator could say that he or she voted for the tax to provide needed money for schools and local governments in his or her district.

Although tax increase votes are difficult ones for legislators, rest assured that from time to time taxes will be raised or new taxes imposed. Some, like the tax on a new Porsche, are very conspicuous. Others, like the gasoline tax, are inconspicuous. But nobody can escape them, not even a teenager hanging around the mall on a Saturday in early spring.

Terry Farmer / Showcase Photography

No one escapes taxes.

Section 3

Citizen Involvement: It Is Your Choice

By Eleanor Meyer and Patrick J. Burns

All eyes were on China in 1989 when college students in the People's Republic of China led massive demonstrations in a struggle to achieve a more democratic form of government. At one point, the demonstrators carried a Chinese model of the Statue of Liberty, a powerful symbol of the hopes and dreams of those who demanded change. The world watched in horror as the government cracked down on the movement, arresting hundreds and killing many of the participants.

People's Republic of China. The name suggests that it is a country where the citizens are in charge, doesn't it? Yet the brutal treatment of the demonstrators reminded us that China is ruled by a Communist government which does not allow dissent to the degree that Americans have come to take for granted.

Indeed, even though the First Amendment to the U.S. Constitution guarantees the right to protest and demonstrate, our government has not always fully protected demonstrators. Union organizers in the 1920s, civil rights demonstrators in the 1950s, and anti-war protesters in the 1960s and 1970s were beaten, jailed, and sometimes killed by the local police or a state's national guard.

That is why it is so important for students to study the federal and state constitutions and to understand and appreciate how much they contribute to our lives. The United States of America is the only democracy with a written constitution that has endured for over 200 years. Just think, the writers did such a good job that we have added only twenty-six amendments. The important thing is that the right to change it and the directions for doing so are built into the document. Our state Constitution is Illinois' fourth. As the state grew and changed, the people exercised their power to change the way our government operates.

You should understand by now that true democracy calls for active participation by its citizens. The U.S. and Illinois constitutions spell out our rights and provide the framework for operating the government, but, in the end, it is the people who must care enough to make it work. History is full of examples of individuals who used power to benefit themselves and their friends instead of to serve the people. It is the informed citizen who knows how to guard against those who would abuse the power entrusted to them. Franklin Delano Roosevelt, a powerful president who held the office longer than any other person, said it this way: "... the only sure bulwark of continuing liberty is a government strong enough to protect the interests of the people, and a people strong enough and well enough informed to maintain its sovereign control over its government" (Fireside Chat, April 14, 1938).

It is easy to sit back and expect government to take care of all our problems. Have you ever heard someone say, "There ought to be a law against it," when complaining about some incident or behavior that offended her or him? Many people are quick to complain but slow to get involved in the process of working for change. Being involved in your government does not necessarily mean that you have to run for class president or student council. You are involved when you cast a vote for someone who holds positions that you favor.

Being involved means expressing your opinion. How do you feel about the U.S. Supreme Court's decision that flag-burning is a legitimate form of protest? Do you think flag-burning goes beyond free speech? Or do you think that the ruling protects citizen rights under the First Amendment? Remember the U.S. Constitution refers to Congress not "abridging the freedom of speech"; "expression" is not found in the Constitution. You probably have strong feelings on the issues of abortion and gun control, too. What do you think of the ideas of withholding a student's driver's license if he or she drops out of school? All of these topics are controversial, and arguments will be heard and decisions will be made by the people who represent you in the state and federal legislatures.

A phone call or letter to your representative is one way of participating in the process. You may think that your voice won't be heard, but when enough citizens express their views, legislators do pay attention. So do governors who must decide to sign or veto legislation that the legislature passes. Remember, they want to be reelected or see candidates succeed them who are of the same party or have similar political attitudes. At the same time, legislators must try to enact policies that will serve the best interests, as they see it, of most citizens most of the time. Public pressure is not always behind the best policies, but citizen pressure does help legislators make decisions on how they will vote on issues.

Here is an example of the way in which public pressure resulted in a major change in your own state government. It may surprise you to learn that until 1981 there were 177 members in Illinois' House of Representatives. Today there are 118 members. The change (known as the cutback amendment) was brought about when Illinois citizens became angry and disgusted with the way in which the legislators had passed pay raises for themselves. Through a process known as initiative and referendum — not an easy process by any means — the voters chose to reduce the size of the Illinois House of Representatives and to require election of its members from single-member districts. They felt that the change would make the lawmakers more accountable and that it would also save the taxpayers money. Many members of the legislature opposed this change; they felt that it would hurt representative government in Illinois. Representatives had been elected for 100 years under a system of three-member districts. That system tended to elect some Republicans in Democratic strongholds and Democrats in Republican strongholds. The system had been devised to almost guarantee that no district could elect three representatives from the same political party.

But the people were angry over those pay raises, and they exercised their power under the Illinois Constitution to amend the Constitution. In the process, the people delivered a strong message to their elected representatives: We don't approve of how you voted yourselves pay raises.

Another argument for participating in government has to do with employment. Most businesses are affected by local, state, or federal regulations in some way. Many business people argue that government should have fewer laws and regulations because they can affect business profits. Many labor people, on the other hand, argue for laws and regulations to protect workers. Teachers, doctors, tavern owners, hairdressers, and operators of bingo games are just a few examples of occupations which are licensed by the state. Many jobs are also created when laws are passed. For example, thousands of employment opportunities exist because of the laws protecting the environment. In addition to government jobs in agencies such as the Environmental Protection Agency, new companies have started up, creating more jobs, to handle such things as recycling products. You can find dozens of examples of jobs which are linked in some way with government.

Approximately one-third of all jobs in the United States are jobs in national, state, or local government. This may surprise you until you consider that most teaching and law enforcement jobs, and many nursing, legal, and scientific jobs as well as secretarial positions involve work in some unit of government. So do jobs involving kitchen help and maintenance work. Construction jobs often depend upon government contracts for buildings and highway projects, and, thus, these workers are indirectly employed by government.

The State Journal-Register

Patrick Quinn (at left) filing petitions on May 1, 1980, at the Illinois State Board of Elections to place the proposed Cutback Amendment to the Illinois Constitution on the general election ballot. The amendment was ratified at the next election, causing the Illinois House to be cut by one-third of its members and to end cumulative voting.

Students in Government

Both the U.S. Congress and the Illinois General Assembly employ a small number of teenagers as pages. Pages are messengers for the legislators when they are in session. You can contact your U.S. congressman or state representative or senator about this opportunity. College graduates who are truly interested in learning more about state government in Illinois can apply for one of the internship programs, such as the Legislative

Staff Internship, in which the student studies and works "inside" government in Springfield.

You have probably heard the expression that you can only get out of something as much as you put into it. That is true of every aspect of life, from the way you do your schoolwork to the way you participate on a ball team. In a democracy such as ours, those words have real meaning. Government can only be as good as the people who are participating in making it work.

This book was written to help you see that there is a direct connection between you and your government. It is not an attempt to convince you that the system works perfectly just because the rules are stated in the constitution. Are there weaknesses in the system? Yes. When decisions are made by our representatives, do some people benefit while others don't? Yes. The system works because we are all bound by the same laws, and constitutions, and it is the people who make it work. Do you have a better idea?

Bill Campbell

Get Involved

If you have not already begun, it is time for you to become involved in political activity and to take some control over what happens to you and to other people. By now you should have developed a reasonably good understanding of the political system in Illinois. There is still much more to learn, and you can learn more through practical experience and more study.

Ask your teacher about starting a Current Issues Club. Meeting with other students to discuss issues is an excellent way to help clarify your political views and develop a deeper understanding of the issues. It is also a way to assemble a group of students who are interested in becoming involved politically. Even though all of you are about the same age, do not be surprised if you find disagreement on issues. Classic disagreements on issues are whether government should pass a law for the "good" of all by taking away some choice of individuals. One example is motorcycle helmet laws. Another classic disagreement is whether government should help a particular category of people by taxing everyone, or at least giving those people a special tax break. For example, it would help a lot of families if the government paid for children's day care while their parents worked. But how do you pay the people caring for the children without raising taxes?

Is your student government organization weak and ineffectual? Could you and other politically aware students in your school change that by running your own candidates for office? In your school, as in the adult community, there will probably be some who only vote occasionally and some who have never voted. If you have never voted, try it. If you don't feel the candidates represent your views, get involved with your friends and find a candidate that does. You have an excellent opportunity to attract students into the system by getting them to vote for your candidate. Find out what you will have to promise to get them to vote. Learn to work within the system to make sure the system works for you.

Students of the sixties were successful in influencing the ending of the war in Vietnam and in establishing more student rights. But their organization did not last because they worked outside and against the system. You can be much more effective working from within. Don't try to do too much, too quickly; limit your goals to ones that are reasonable, important, and obtainable. Don't expect to get everything you want; remember that politics involves the art of compromise. If you don't want to run for office, become active in electing someone who shares your ideas.

Get a group of students to attend school board meetings. In Chicago, attend your local school council meeting. Wherever your school is located in Illinois, the school board meetings are open for all to attend. You may not always find them exciting, but you will learn how school policy is made. Take note of influential board members, and, if you can detect a split in the board, make note of this. It can be useful when there is to be a vote on an issue vital to your group. Convince your parents and neighbors to attend board meetings and get them involved. If you want to become a political activist, get involved to help reelect board members with whom you agree and to defeat those with whom you disagree strongly.

When you are a senior, you must avoid a natural tendency to become less involved since you feel that you will not be around to enjoy any gains that are made. You may be interested in adding a new course in the curriculum, but don't work for it because you know you won't be around to take it. You should rise above this selfishness and keep in mind that others will benefit.

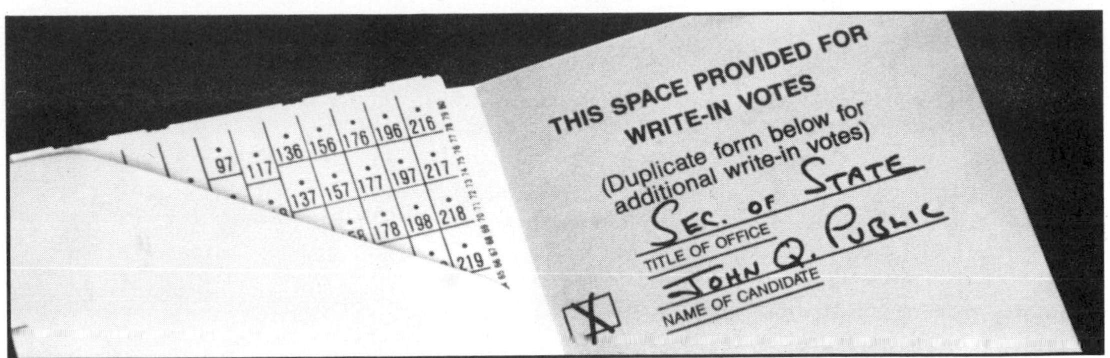

Illinois State Board of Elections

Most voting is done by a metal styllus on a punchcard ballot, but there are provisions for writing in candidates not on the ballot. The ballot pictured above shows how to correctly "write in" a candidate for a government office. If not done correctly, your "write in" vote will not be counted.

Don't hesitate to get involved in political activity outside the school. Attend a city council meeting or another local government meeting. You may be able to organize a school-sponsored trip to Springfield to watch the state legislature in action. You don't have to go to Washington, D.C., to see the U.S. Congress in action. You can watch the U.S. Congress live on C-SPAN on television. (If you do not get C-SPAN on your TV at home, see if your teacher can have it taped for school.)

At some point you need to make a decision concerning which political party best represents your views and interests. Some people remain "independents," but the political parties make the nominations for president, members of Congress, governor and other state-elected officials, and sometimes local officials. You will probably find that neither Republicans nor Democrats represent your views exactly. There are different views within each party, but there are central tendencies for each. On balance, there is a difference between the Republican and Democratic parties, yet in campaigns, candidates of both parties often seek to win the "middle of the road" voters. You need to choose the one closest to your views, or perhaps you may find yourself more comfortable with being an independent. There are other, more minor political parties. There is no law against establishing new political parties. These "third" parties have not been effective in the past, but you may be the person who will change all of that.

Herald and Review

A wooden folding chair, with Old Glory and a sign taped to it, marks the Ward 2 polling place in Assumption. All other signs must be 100 feet away from a polling place.

If you decide to join a political party, you should seek your Republican or Democrat precinct committee person and offer your services to help in election campaigns. Don't expect to be put in a position of great responsibility and influence. Realize that you will have to "pay your dues" by doing a lot of busy work. You will probably begin by running errands or stuffing envelopes. Whatever job you do, you are learning more about the system, while you are getting to know politicians and they are getting to know you.

You may also wish to get involved in a neighborhood organization or in a special interest group. There are always problems to resolve and your chances of doing something are greater as part of a group.

If you continue your education in college, you can get involved working for the party there or working in a group on a college or national issue. You should also get involved in your student government at college.

Once you have gone to work, you will have the opportunity to get involved in political activity in your union, professional or business organization. You may not want to work in politics as a profession, but you should always stay involved. Be ready to participate in rallies or demonstrations, write letters, make phone calls, sign petitions, and donate a little money to support causes in which you believe.

On your eighteenth birthday, be sure you take the first step to join our representative system of government: Register to vote. There's no fee and no test to take. If you don't know where to register, ask your parents or teacher.

Authors

Patrick J. Burns, a counselor and humanities instructor at Shelbyville High School for twenty-seven years, also has taught social studies part-time for Lake Land Community College in Mattoon for twenty-four years. A graduate of Southern Illinois University at Carbondale, he received his B.S. in 1957 and his M.S. in 1959. He has done other graduate work at Eastern Illinois University, Illinois State University, and the University of Illinois. He credits much of his understanding of Illinois state government to his family's discussions when he was growing up in the coal mining area of Williamson County, particularly from his Aunt Agnes Burns Wieck and her husband Edward Wieck.

Darlene Emmert Fisher, social studies teacher at New Trier Township High School in Winnetka (1963-69, 1979-90), previously taught eighth grade social studies at St. Francis Xavier School in Wilmette (1975-76). She received her A.B. in 1962 from Albion College and her M.A. in 1963 from the University of Pennsylvania. A resident of Evanston, she is a member of the board of the League of Women Voters of Evanston. She has published several articles in various periodicals, including a biweekly column for the *Evanston Review* (1979-82).

Michael D. Klemens, Statehouse bureau chief in Springfield for *Illinois Issues* magazine since 1986, previously taught eighth grade English and social studies in New York at Ogdensburg Free Academy (1972-73). He received his A.B. from Dartmouth College in 1971 and his M.A. from Sangamon State University in 1986. He lives in Springfield and is an expert on state finances.

Eleanor Meyer, a teacher at Beardstown Junior High School, has taught eighth grade U.S. history for six years and seventh grade geography since 1964. She received her B.A. in elementary education from George Washington University in 1956 and her M.A. in U.S. history from Western Illinois University in 1982.

Denny L. Shillings has been a social studies teacher at Homewood-Flossmoor High School since 1973. Before that he taught at Sheldon High School and Edwards County High School in Albion. He received his A.A. from Wabash Valley College in Mount Carmel in 1967, his B.S. in education from Eastern Illinois University in 1969, and his M.A. in history from Eastern Illinois University in 1972. He has also done post-graduate work at Chicago State University, Governors State University, Illinois State University, and Northern Illinois University. He is the author of *The Living Constitution,* published by Glencoe/McGraw-Hill Publishing Co. (1990) and has been contributor, consultant, or editor for other publications on history, social studies, and economics. He is affiliated with several professional associations and in 1989-90 served on the executive committee of the National Council for the Social Studies.

Judy Lee (Lewis) Uphoff, principal of Lovington High School, was a social studies teacher for twenty years. She received her B.S. in education in 1969 and her M.S. in education in 1972, both from Eastern Illinois University. She is a contributing author to *Understanding the Illinois Constitution,* published by the Illinois Bar Foundation in 1986, and she was a government intern for Illinois state Rep. Mike Tate.

Editors

Dr. James M. Banovetz is professor and director, Division of Public Administration, Department of Political Science, Northern Illinois University, and a member of the *Illinois Issues* board.

Caroline A. Gherardini is editor of *Illinois Issues,* published by Sangamon State University and cosponsored by the University of Illinois.

Resources

The 1990-1991 Handbook of Illinois Government, published by the Illinois Office of the Secretary of State. Available free from your Illinois regional superintendent of education.

Includes the U.S. and Illinois constitutions; the basics for each branch of government, including descriptions of major executive agencies, the Illinois court system, and the legislative process. Includes the names and photographs of all elected Illinois state officers, and state maps showing districts for the legislative and judicial branches.

Illinois State Highway Map, printed by the Illinois Department of Transportation. Available free (although bulk orders are filled based on quantities available) by writing to:
Office of Public Affairs
Illinois Department of Transportation
2300 South Dirksen Parkway
Springfield, Illinois 62764

Available at your library, bookstore, or from the publisher:

A New Game Plan for Illinois, by James D. Nowlan, published by Neltnor House in Chicago.
Basic Illinois Government: A Systematic Explanation, by David Kenney, published by Southern Illinois University Press in Carbondale, Illinois.
Historic Illinois from the Air, by David Buisseret (illustrations and cartography by Tom Willcockson), published by the University of Chicago Press.
Home Rule in Illinois: Image and Reality, by James M. Banovetz and Thomas W. Kelty, published by *Illinois Issues* at Sangamon State University in Springfield, Illinois.
Illinois Issues, monthly magazine published by Sangamon State University in Springfield, Illinois.
Illinois Local Government: A Handbook, edited by James F. Keane and Gary Koch, published by Southern Illinois University Press in Carbondale, Illinois.
Lawmaking in Illinois: Legislative Politics, People and Processes, by Jack R. Van Der Slik and Kent D. Redfield, published by *Illinios Issues* at Sangamon State University in Springfield, Illinois.
Understanding the Illinois Constitution, by Frank Kopecky and Mary Sherman Harris, published by the Illinois Bar Foundation in Springfield, Illinois.

Forthcoming:

Book. *Illinois Government and Politics,* by Samuel K. Gove and James D. Nowlan, to be published by the University of Nebraska Press in Lincoln.
Video. *Have All Voted Who Wish,* produced by Joe Howard, J.P. Communications, Chicago, Illinois.

Illustration Credits

During the course of collecting and identifying photographs, cartoons, and other artwork for this textbook, many people have been very generous with their time and talents to make the graphics as interesting and as accurate as possible. The editors appreciate their assistance and acknowledge the contributions of these individuals, agencies, companies, and organizations.

Aging, Illinois Department on, for photographs, 19, 53.
Alcoholism and Substance Abuse, Illinois Department of, for photograph, 54.
Barnard, Jay, Senate Republican Staff, for photographs, 42, 44.
Bell, Frank, *The Sentinel,* Illiopolis, Illinois, for photograph, 70.
Bridge's Amoco, Springfield, Illinois, for permission to take photographs on their premises, 85.
Cadagin, Richard J., Judge, Seventh Judicial Circuit, for the mock scenes in his courtroom, 59.
Campbell, Bill, for cartoons from *Campbell Cartoon Service: The Last Cartoons* (copyright 1980), 4, 5, 8, 9, 24, 32, 33, 39, 42, 43, 55, 62, 74, 92.
Caterpillar Inc., Decatur, Illinois, for photograph, 32.
Chicago Tribune, for reprint of copyrighted photograph, 79.
Conservation, Illinois Department of, for photographs, 18, 53, 81, 83, 86, 88.
Corrections, Illinois Department of, for photograph, 18.
D.A.R.E. Bureau, Illinois State Police, for photograph, 14.
Davis, Sam, House Democratic Staff, Illinois General Assembly, for photographs, 39, 42, 43.
Dudycz, Sen. Walter, for permission to use photo printed in *Chicago Tribune,* 79.
Education, Illinois State Board of, for artwork, 9, 13, 19, 36, 37.
Elections, Illinois State Board of, for artwork and photograph, 9, 93.
Farmer, Terry, Showcase Photography, for contributing his time in taking so many photographs especially for the textbook, 14, 16, 17, 18, 19, 21, 25, 29, 30, 31, 38, 52, 55, 59, 60, 67, 71, 76, 83, 85, 89.
Fenton, Jack, for his cooperation in illustrating township government, 70.
Foreman, Bill, Silver Images Photography, for photograph that appears on the cover and again on page 6.
Fremon, David K., for photographs, 72, 73.
Governor's Office, for photographs, 41, 48, 51.
Hagen, Bill, Chief Photographer for *The State Journal-Register,* for his assistance in providing photographs and cartoons.
Havener, Les, for his cooperation in illustrating township government, 70.
Herald and Review, Decatur, Illinois, for photographs, 23, 93.
Hippler, Charles E., Public Affairs Manager, Caterpillar Inc., Decatur, Illinois, for his cooperation in illustrating the connection between businesses and the community, 32.
House Democratic Staff, Illinois General Assembly, for photographs, 39, 42, 43.
House Republican Staff, Illinois General Assembly, for photograph, 44.
Illinois Environmental Protection Agency, for photographs, 20, 30.
Illinois Army National Guard, for photographs, 27, 50.
Illinois Historic Preservation Agency, for photographs, 56.
Illinois State Police, for photographs, 14, 16, 29.
Illinois Supreme Court, for photograph, 61.
Isringhausen Imports, Springfield, Illinois, for allowing photographs to be taken in their showroom, 85.
Jones, Kevin, Senate Democratic Staff, Illinois General Assembly, for photographs, 12, 40, 43.
Koenigsaecher, Jim, House Republican Staff, Illinois General Assembly, for photograph, 44.
Legislative Research Unit, Illinois General Assembly, for map and chart, 2, 46.
Lincoln Library, Springfield, Illinois, and the Sangamon Valley Collection of historical photographs housed at the library, for loan of photographs, 3, 7, 76.
Locher, Barry, Assistant Managing Editor for *The State Journal-Register,* for all his assistance in providing photographs and artwork.
McCredie, Roger, Illinois Department of Transportation, for photographs, 18, 52, 68, 84, 88.
Michaelson, Ronald D., Executive Director, State Board of Elections, for permission to reprint chart, 5.
Paulus, Dick, for permission to use cartoons, 4, 12, 24, 40, 42, 50, 53, 57, 74, 82, 86, 87.
Penne, Joseph C., Public Affairs Representative, Caterpillar Inc., Decatur, Illinois, for his assistance in accurately describing photograph, 32.
Public Aid, Illinois Department of, for photographs, 15, 53.
Randolph, Jon, Jon Randolph Photography, for permission to reprint photos, 31, 70.

Roberts, Bud, Illinois Army National Guard, for photographs, 27, 50.
Rogers, Jim, House Democratic Staff, Illinois General Assembly, for photographs, 39, 42, 43.
Roth, Thomas, D.A.R.E. Bureau of Illinois State Police, for photograph, 14.
Russo, Ed, Head of Sangamon Valley Collection, Lincoln Library, Springfield, Illinois, for his assistance in using photographs from the Collection, 3, 7, 76.
Sangamon Valley Collection, see Lincoln Library.
Schultz, Don, Director of Election Operations, State Board of Elections, for photograph, 93.
Scobell, Georgia A., for photograph, 69.
Szczepaniak, James J., Public Information Officer, Village of Skokie, for his cooperation in illustrating municipal government, 71, 79.
Senate Democratic Staff, Illinois General Assembly, for photographs, 12, 40, 43.
Senate Republican Staff, Illinois General Assembly, for photographs, 42, 44.
Skokie, Village of, for photographs, 71, 79.
State Journal-Register, for photographs and artwork, 1, 8, 10, 11, 20, 21, 25, 26, 34, 45, 48, 55, 73, 75, 77, 79, 80, 81, 84, 91; and for permission to use photographs in the Sangamon Valley Collection, Lincoln Library, 3, 7, 76.
Thompson, Mike, for cartoons published originally in *The State Journal-Register,* 1, 8, 10, 21, 45, 48, 55, 73, 77, 84.
Transportation, Illinois Department of, for photographs and chart, 18, 52, 68, 84, 88.
Tonge, David C., for photograph, 56.
White Oaks Mall, Springfield, Illinois, for permission to take photographs on their premises, 67, 85, 89.
White Oaks Mall Shoppers. A special thanks to all our Mall Shoppers, who helped us illustrate Chapter Eight: **Nick Bilbrey, Stephenie Chick, Kristina Karrick, Bill Keleher, Kim Krepel, Brandon Pickel, Matt Robinson, Sunny Scobell, and Heather Wright.**
Whitler, Albert W., for his assistance in describing the Macoupin County courthouse, 69.

Index

References to illustrations are printed in boldface type.